No. 73447

FOUR MILE POLYCHROME BOWL
Greatest diameter, 34.1 cm.
Homolovi (No. 1), Arizona

ANASAZI PAINTED POTTERY
IN
FIELD MUSEUM OF NATURAL HISTORY

BY

PAUL S. MARTIN
CHIEF CURATOR, DEPARTMENT OF ANTHROPOLOGY

AND

ELIZABETH S. WILLIS

ANTHROPOLOGY, MEMOIRS

FIELD MUSEUM OF NATURAL HISTORY

VOLUME 5

DECEMBER 31, 1940

KRAUS REPRINT CO.
Millwood, New York
1977

The Library of Congress Cataloged the First Issue
of this title as follows:

Martin, Paul Sidney, 1899-

Anasazi painted pottery in Field museum of natural history, by Paul S. Martin . . . and Elizabeth S. Willis . . . [Chi-
cago, Field museum press] 1940.

1 p. l., 5-284 p. incl. illus. (map) 125 pl. (incl. front.) 32 cm. (Anthropology, Memoirs. Field museum of natural history. v. 5)

Descriptive letterpress on versos facing plates.
Bibliography: p. 271-274.

1. Indians of North America—Pottery.   2. Pueblo Indians—Art. 3.
Pueblo Indians—Antiq.   I. Willis, Elizabeth S., joint author.   II.
Title.

E98.P8M3   970.6738   41—11775

ISBN 0-527-61900-0

Reprinted with permission of the Field Museum of Natural History
KRAUS REPRINT CO.
A U.S. Division of Kraus-Thomson Organization Limited

Printed in U.S.A.

CONTENTS

ANASAZI PAINTED POTTERY

IN

FIELD MUSEUM OF NATURAL HISTORY

INTRODUCTION

Early in 1939, we decided to sort typologically the 5,000 unbroken specimens of painted Anasazi (Basket Maker-Pueblo) pottery in the collection of Field Museum. Since its accession the collection has been in storage and we hoped by means of a typological sorting to make this material useful and productive. By utilizing the data collected by modern archaeologists, we could allot to the varied wares a cultural relationship and a relative chronological order.

After the preliminaries of thorough water and acid baths for each piece, came the rough color sorting; that is, the whites were separated from the yellows, the reds, and the polychromes. When this had been accomplished we discovered that the collection was remarkably comprehensive and we decided that a publication of representative pieces would be a useful contribution to the literature of Anasazi archaeology.

We found that about 95 per cent of our collection was secured during the 1880's and 1890's when cow-men, ranchers, and antiquarians did a tremendous amount of digging in the regions of Arizona, Utah, Colorado, and New Mexico. At that time, there existed no Federal law for the preservation of antiquities, and digging was unrestrained and unhindered. Some of it was done on picnics, some for profit, and some for the fun of gathering "relics" of the "Aztecs"—the name by which many of the early settlers referred to the Pueblo Indians. As a result of such indiscriminate collecting, much of our pottery was undocumented. Only the site from which the collection came, the collector's name, and the date of purchase were known. The specimens were catalogued merely as Southwestern pottery, or "ancient dishes from Arizona." In those early days, few bothered their heads about pottery types or chronological differences.

Since then the archaeological horizon has broadened; taxonomy has been introduced to the profession; and systematizing of knowledge has begun.

Methodology and classification are justifiable when used with restraint, and when accompanied by a sense of balance and a leavening humor. With this precaution in mind, we classified our collection and selected representative pieces for publication. Data previously accumulated with great care and reported by a score or more of well-trained archaeologists, and classifications evolved from time and cultural relationships helped immeasurably in the work of analyzing our collection.

This analysis completed, we selected approximately 900 vessels illustrating most of the major Anasazi painted pottery types, many of which were previously known only from photographs of potsherds, or, at best, of single specimens.

The illustrations of these specimens now may be minutely studied and leisurely examined. This "armchair approach" facilitates study of this pottery, and enables the individual to correlate the substance gained from allied archaeological reports with the specimens pictured here.

Visualization of pottery types through the medium of the written word is frequently difficult, as meanings and connotations vary with the individual. Seeing the specimen overcomes the limitations of written description. Purposely then, our text is sparse.

We illustrate not only the finest specimens of each pottery type in the collection, but also all seldom-published variants in technique, design, and shape which are representative of our collection of each given type. For example, an individual interested in the range of design or shapes of pottery from the Kayenta region, can see most of the Kayenta types by referring to the pages devoted to them.

This volume should be helpful not only to archaeologists and other workers in Southwestern archaeology, but also to students and teachers of art, for the Pueblo potter was adept at securing richness, variety, and ingenuity of design, and incorporating them in varied shapes and forms.

In the classification of pottery types, we have proceeded without the use of petrographic analysis. Although much of the modern literature of pottery depends on this method, it was not adaptable to whole vessels.

Some will not agree with a few of our typological assignments; others may dislike the pottery names used in this volume, and may object to the Gladwin method employed in the organization and publication of this material.

The Gladwin system charts the proven as well as supposed chronological and cultural relationships of the ancient Southwest.

PRIMARY CULTURAL RELATIONSHIPS IN GLADWIN'S CLASSIFICATION (SIMPLIFIED)

(Pottery types pp. 141–163)	(Pottery types pp. 164–257)	(Pottery types pp. 259–269)	(Pottery types pp. 11–123)	(Pottery types pp. 125–139)
Chaco Branch	Cibola Branch	Salado Branch	Kayenta Branch	Mesa Verde Branch

Little Colorado Stem

San Juan Stem

(Anasazi) Basket Maker Root

This classification is an attempt to correlate the archaeological findings in this area, and to supply a framework for further developments in this field. Modifications of the relationships implied by the Gladwins have been made from time to time, yet these changes have in no way altered the original purpose of the system.

A parallel exists in regard to this volume. The Gladwin method commended itself to us because it was flexible enough to meet the demands of our collection. Also, it afforded us a logical and convenient system of arranging our illustrations. The photographs will be useful for study, and may be reclassified according to any system the reader wishes to use. The provenience for each vessel is correct, and the chronological allotment reasonably so. We have tried to make only major distinctions of the types in our collection.

In order to facilitate the use of this catalogue, we have included the following:

(1) A map (p. 10) of part of the Southwest, showing practically every site mentioned in this report. Locations are, for the most part, accurate; some—found only in old publications and on old maps—may show a slight error.

(2) A bibliography (p. 271), which includes all references employed in sorting out our pottery by branches. Added, of course, is a listing of all references used in compiling this volume (p. 272).

(3) A table (p. 275) of all major sites represented in this volume, with references to the photographed specimens from those locations. This will be helpful to those who prefer the site division as a unit in the study of pottery.

(4) A numerical index (p. 280) of the illustrated specimens, with collectors' names appended.

(5) An alphabetical index (p. 281) including the names of most sub-types and synonyms for illustrated types, as well as the type-names used in this volume. This should be of value to those confused, as we were, by the fact that there may be five or six names for one pottery type; some of these names go back in the literature from thirty to fifty years.

Much of the pottery illustrated has not been seen by layman, student, or specialist since its excavation and transfer to Field Museum. By making these photographs of approximately one-sixth of our pottery available to others, and by presenting all types, variations, and differences in design and shape, we believe we have launched this collection into a new era of usefulness.

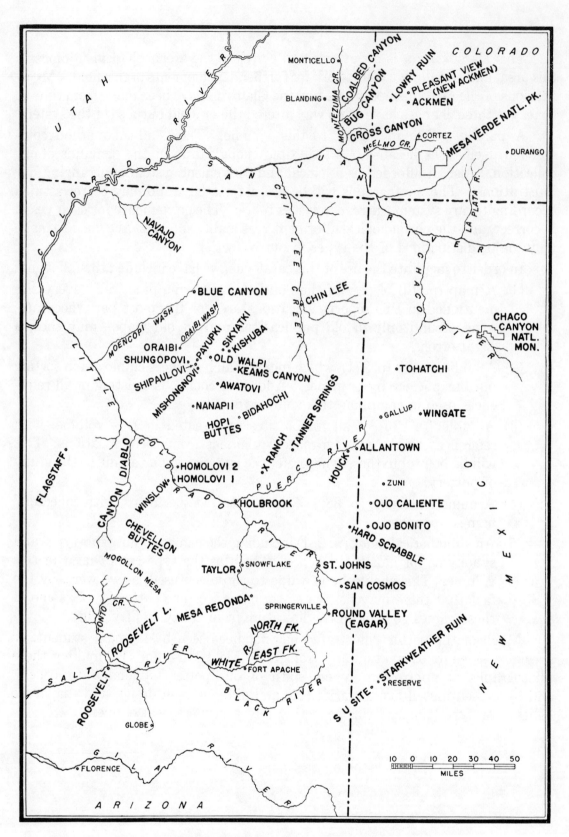

MAP SHOWING LOCATION OF SITES

I. KAYENTA BRANCH

The pottery classified as of the Kayenta Branch is scattered over most of northeastern Arizona; that is, roughly from the Lukachukai Mountains west to Grand Canyon, south to Flagstaff and east towards Gallup, where it is intermixed with pottery of the Chaco Branch. The areas of greatest concentration are near Marsh Pass (Arizona) and in the Hopi country (near Keams Canyon and vicinity). Pieces, both early and late, traveled (probably by trade) far beyond the rough boundaries just given.

This branch is named for the town of Kayenta, Arizona, in the vicinity of which the first known pottery representative of this branch was found.

The paint on all the Black-on-Whites of this series, except Bidahochi Black-on-White, is probably organic.

The evolution of design motifs is easily traced from the earliest to the latest Black-on-White potteries (about A.D. 700–1300). During this interval of about six centuries, there were five distinct Black-on-White types: Kana-a, Black Mesa, Tusayan, Sagi, and Bidahochi. The designs on Bidahochi are transitional from Sagi Black-on-White to Jeddito Black-on-Orange.

Fortunately our collection includes a number of whole Kana-a Black-on-White specimens showing shapes and variations of designs never before so fully illustrated. Deserving of special attention in the Kana-a Black-on-White series are one mug and three bottles with long, narrow necks which, so far as we know, have never before been mentioned.

By examining the designs on the Kana-a and the Black Mesa Black-on-White series, it will be evident that there is a similarity between these designs and those on Red Mesa Black-on-White pottery (Chaco Branch, Plates 66–67).

We have observed that there is no clear connection, so far as designs are concerned, between Lino Black-on-Gray and Kana-a Black-on-White. Furthermore, the latter is slipped and smoothly polished, while the former never is. Yet Kana-a Black-on-White succeeds Lino Black-on-Gray in this region. Why was there no carryover? We do not know. Our guess is that the techniques of slipping, polishing, and utilization of certain designs (solids bordered by fine lines, common in Kana-a Black-on-White, White Mound Black-on-White and Red Mesa Black-on-White) came from the south and are suggestive, except for base-color and type of paint, of Mogollon Red-on-Brown pottery. Although this is only a guess, it may be worth following up some time by means of excavations.

It would seem, on a typological basis, that Sikyatki Polychrome degenerated before the advent of the Spaniards. We feel that this is true because a substantial portion of this collection represents the poor workmanship of Post-Conquest pottery, but with no trace of Spanish influence on the designs. The recent excavations of Mr. J. O. Brew at Awatovi should help to clear up this point.

It has interested us to note that the continuum of culture from ancient to modern times as reflected in the pottery of this branch is clearer than elsewhere in our studies. We can trace the ancestry of this pottery, with scarcely a break, from modern Hopi pottery back to Kana-a Black-on-White—an interval of approximately 1,200 years. This connection between the modern Hopi Indians and their prehistoric relatives is clear in our typological studies on this series and is substantiated by the juxtaposition of modern Hopi towns, towns occupied at the time of the Pueblo Revolt (1680), and more ancient ones.

The Kayenta pottery types illustrated in this publication are generally dated as follows:

	Estimated date A. D.		Estimated date A. D.
Kana-a Black-on-White	700–850	Sagi Black-on-White	1200–1300
Black Mesa Black-on-White	875–1150	Bidahochi Black-on-White	1325–1400
Tusayan Black-on-White	1100–1275	Jeddito Black-on-Orange	1200–1300
Tusayan Black-on-Red	850–1125	Jeddito Black-on-Yellow	1325–1600
Tusayan Polychrome	1150–1300	Bidahochi Polychrome	1300–1400
Kayenta Polychrome	1150–1300	Sikyatki Polychrome	1400–1625*
Kiet Siel Polychrome	1150–1300		

* And copies made at present.

PLATE 2: KANA-A BLACK-ON-WHITE

Kayenta Branch

FIGURE 1: No. 80063

> *Description:* Bottle; lug handles perforated vertically.
> *Dimension:* Greatest height, 14 cm.
> *Provenience:* Chukubi (one mile northeast of Shipaulovi), Arizona.

FIGURE 2: No. 66685

> *Description:* Pitcher; lateral flattening.
> *Dimension:* Greatest height, 14.2 cm.
> *Provenience:* Near Blue Canyon, Arizona.

FIGURE 3: No. 75110

> *Description:* Seed jar; lug handles perforated vertically. Unusually thin walls.
> *Dimension:* Greatest height, including handles, 20.1 cm.
> *Provenience:* North of Holbrook, Arizona.

FIGURE 4: No. 66632

> *Description:* Bottle; lug handles perforated vertically.
> *Dimension:* Greatest height, 21.2 cm.
> *Provenience:* Near Oraibi, Arizona.

FIGURE 5: No. 66633

> *Description:* Pitcher; handle missing.
> *Dimension:* Greatest height, 17.1 cm.
> *Provenience:* Shungopovi, Arizona.

1

2

3

4

5

PLATE 3: KANA-A BLACK-ON-WHITE
Kayenta Branch

FIGURE 1: No. 81557
> *Description:* Gourd-shaped vessel.
> *Dimension:* Greatest height, 15.6 cm.
> *Provenience:* Chaco Canyon, New Mexico.

FIGURE 2: No. 81854
> *Description:* Pitcher; flat-bottomed.
> *Dimension:* Greatest height, 12 cm.
> *Provenience:* Chaco Canyon, New Mexico.

FIGURE 3: No. 75109
> *Description:* Mug; flat-bottomed.   Glossy white finish.
> *Dimension:* Greatest height, including handle, 7.9 cm.
> *Provenience:* Two miles north of Holbrook, Arizona.

FIGURE 4: No. 66688
> *Description:* Jar; egg-shaped.   Another specimen of Kana-a Black-on-White in our collection has a similar shape but with vertical sides and flattish base.
> *Dimension:* Greatest height, 10.6 cm.
> *Provenience:* Ruins near Shipaulovi, Arizona.

FIGURE 5: No. 66674
> *Description:* Pitcher; dull gray finish.
> *Dimension:* Greatest height, 19.2 cm.
> *Provenience:* Near Blue Canyon, Arizona.

FIGURE 6: No. 21107
> *Description:* Bottle; lug-handles perforated vertically.
> *Dimension:* Greatest height, 22.2 cm.
> *Provenience:* Hopi country, Arizona.

1

2

3

4

5

6

PLATE 4: KANA-A BLACK-ON-WHITE
Kayenta Branch

FIGURE 1: No. 66700

Description: Bowl; the only one in the collection of this type with exterior decoration.
Dimension: Greatest diameter, 21.6 cm.
Provenience: Near Mishongnovi, Arizona.

FIGURE 2: No. 66644

Description: Bowl; vertical handle.
Dimension: Greatest diameter, excluding handle, 17.8 cm.
Provenience: Three miles northeast of Oraibi, Arizona.

FIGURE 3: No. 74670

Description: Pitcher; double-ribbed handle.
Dimension: Greatest height, 10.2 cm.
Provenience: Bidahochi, Arizona.

FIGURE 4: No. 74683

Description: Bowl; bright white finish on interior, Fugitive Red on exterior.
Dimension: Greatest diameter, 17.7 cm.
Provenience: Bidahochi, Arizona.

FIGURE 5: No. 81388

Description: Pitcher; duck-effigy shape.   Type uncertain.
Dimension: Greatest height, 11.7 cm.
Provenience: Kishuba, Arizona.

FIGURE 6: No. 21429

Description: Bowl; very crude, but has carbon paint.   Type uncertain.
Dimension: Greatest diameter, 19.5 cm.
Provenience: Uncertain.

FIGURE 7: No. 21053

Description: Bowl; very crude, but has carbon paint.   Type uncertain.
Dimension: Greatest diameter, 18.8 cm.
Provenience: Hopi country, Arizona.

FIGURE 8: No. 81074

Description: Bowl; unusually thick walls.   Type uncertain.
Dimension: Greatest diameter, 17.5 cm.
Provenience: Old Walpi, Arizona.

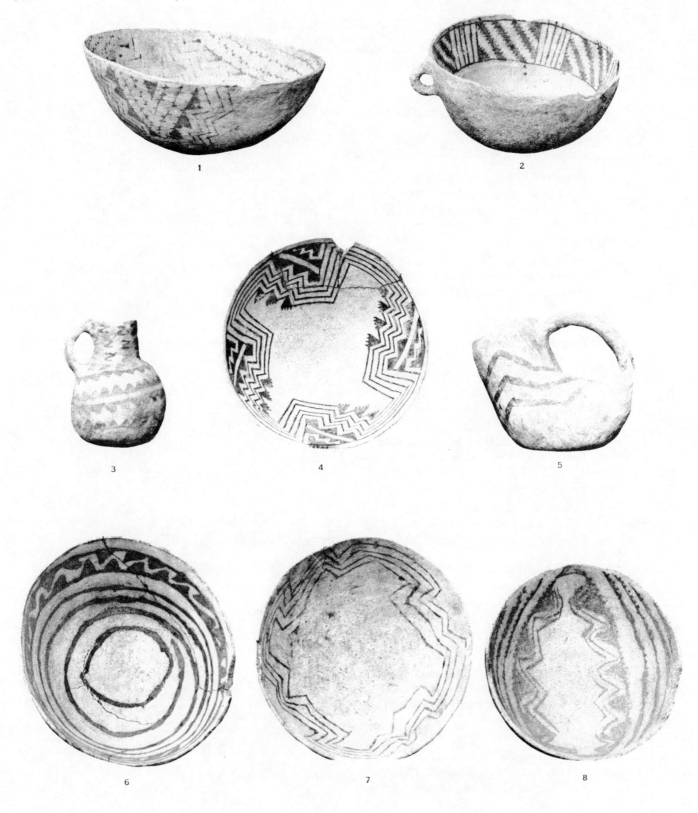

PLATE 5: BLACK MESA BLACK-ON-WHITE

Kayenta Branch

FIGURE 1: No. 66641

Description: Pitcher; glossy finish.
Dimension: Greatest height, 12.6 cm.
Provenience: Oraibi, Arizona.

FIGURE 2: No. 81928

Description: Pitcher. Type uncertain.
Dimension: Greatest height, 9.4 cm.
Provenience: Lower Little Colorado River(?), Arizona.

FIGURE 3: No. 66643

Description: Pitcher. Type uncertain.
Dimension: Greatest height, 13.1 cm.
Provenience: Three miles northeast of Oraibi, Arizona.

FIGURE 4: No. 44218

Description: Seed jar; two pairs of perforations in rim for carrying-cord.
Dimension: Greatest height, 10.7 cm.
Provenience: Hopi country, Arizona.

FIGURE 5: No. 66696

Description: Seed Jar.
Dimension: Greatest height, 11.6 cm.
Provenience: One mile south of Payupki, Arizona.

FIGURE 6: No. 82007

Description: Seed jar.
Dimension: Greatest height, 9.9 cm.
Provenience: Little Colorado Valley, probably below Winslow, Arizona.

FIGURE 7: No. 74573

Description: Pitcher; body nearly globular.
Dimension: Greatest height, 13.7 cm.
Provenience: Ojo Caliente, New Mexico.

FIGURE 8: No. 66681

Description: Pitcher; unusual low-bulging shape.
Dimension: Greatest height, 13.9 cm.
Provenience: Just south of Mishongnovi, Arizona.

FIGURE 9: No. 72908

Description: Pitcher.
Dimension: Greatest height, 13.3 cm.
Provenience: Homolovi (No. 1), Arizona.

1

2

3

4

5

6

7

8

9

PLATE 6: BLACK MESA BLACK-ON-WHITE

Kayenta Branch

FIGURE 1: No. 82036

> *Description:* Bowl; steep sided.
> *Dimension:* Greatest diameter, 14.2 cm.
> *Provenience:* Little Colorado Valley, probably below Winslow, Arizona.

FIGURE 2: No. 75240

> *Description:* Bowl.
> *Dimension:* Greatest diameter, 19.2 cm.
> *Provenience:* Sikyatki, Arizona.

FIGURE 3: No. 74143

> *Description:* Bowl.
> *Dimension:* Greatest diameter, 14.8 cm.
> *Provenience:* San Cosmos, Arizona.

FIGURE 4: No. 66682

> *Description:* Bowl.
> *Dimension:* Greatest diameter, 17.3 cm.
> *Provenience:* Just south of Mishongnovi, Arizona.

FIGURE 5: No. 81544

> *Description:* Bowl; warped.
> *Dimension:* Greatest diameter, 25.2 cm.
> *Provenience:* Chaco Canyon, New Mexico.

FIGURE 6: No. 81817

> *Description:* Bowl; very shiny paint.
> *Dimension:* Greatest diameter, 16.8 cm.
> *Provenience:* Chaco Canyon, New Mexico.

FIGURE 7: No. 82034

> *Description:* Bowl; paint polished to gray.
> *Dimension:* Greatest diameter, 18.2 cm.
> *Provenience:* Little Colorado Valley, probably below Winslow, Arizona.

FIGURE 8: No. 74786

> *Description:* Bowl; warped even more than shown in photograph.
> *Dimension:* Greatest diameter, 27.3 cm.
> *Provenience:* X Ranch, Arizona.

FIGURE 9: No. 75241

> *Description:* Bowl.
> *Dimension:* Greatest diameter, 20.1 cm.
> *Provenience:* Sikyatki, Arizona.

PLATE 7: BLACK MESA BLACK-ON-WHITE
Kayenta Branch

FIGURE 1: No. 82035
> *Description:* Bowl; bright white finish.
> *Dimension:* Greatest diameter, 15.5 cm.
> *Provenience:* Little Colorado Valley, probably below Winslow, Arizona.

FIGURE 2: No. 81552
> *Description:* Bowl; flat rim, design, and diagonal hachure of the Chaco, but carbon
> paint of the Kayenta. Type uncertain.
> *Dimension:* Greatest diameter, 20.2 cm.
> *Provenience:* Chaco Canyon, New Mexico.

FIGURE 3: No. 81630
> *Description:* Bowl; paint has a blue cast.
> *Dimension:* Greatest diameter, 15.7 cm.
> *Provenience:* Navajo Canyon, Arizona.

FIGURE 4: No. 81984
> *Description:* Bowl; very rough finish. Note double-loop horizontal handle.
> *Dimension:* Greatest diameter, excluding handle, 13.2 cm.
> *Provenience:* Lower Little Colorado River(?), Arizona.

FIGURE 5: No. 81303
> *Description:* Bowl; unusual in-curving rim.
> *Dimension:* Greatest diameter, 14.8 cm.
> *Provenience:* Kishuba, Arizona.

FIGURE 6: No. 82026
> *Description:* Bowl; vertical handle.
> *Dimension:* Greatest diameter, excluding handle, 12.9 cm.
> *Provenience:* Little Colorado Valley, probably below Winslow, Arizona.

FIGURE 7: No. 81816
> *Description:* Bowl; very smooth interior finish.
> *Dimension:* Greatest diameter, 16.6 cm.
> *Provenience:* Chaco Canyon, New Mexico.

FIGURE 8: No. 81996
> *Description:* Bowl.
> *Dimension:* Greatest diameter, 20.5 cm.
> *Provenience:* Lower Little Colorado(?), Arizona.

FIGURE 9: No. 81065
> *Description:* Bowl; thick, clear slip. Thickness of slip can easily be seen where it has
> flaked away from the hole.
> *Dimension:* Greatest diameter, 18 cm.
> *Provenience:* Old Walpi, Arizona.

PLATE 8: BLACK MESA BLACK-ON-WHITE
Kayenta Branch

FIGURE 1: No. 74666
> *Description:* Jar; wide-mouthed. Two pairs of holes in rim for carrying-cord.
> *Dimension:* Greatest height, 8.6 cm.
> *Provenience:* Bidahochi, Arizona.

FIGURE 2: No. 81373
> *Description:* Mug; similar to later mugs of Mesa Verde.
> *Dimension:* Greatest height, 5.5 cm.
> *Provenience:* Oraibi Wash, Arizona.

FIGURE 3: No. 81973
> *Description:* Seed jar; miniature.
> *Dimension:* Greatest height, 4.8 cm.
> *Provenience:* Lower Little Colorado(?), Arizona.

FIGURE 4: No. 81326
> *Description:* Colander. This is early for this shape.
> *Dimension:* Greatest height, 6.8 cm.
> *Provenience:* Kishuba, Arizona.

FIGURE 5: No. 21060
> *Description:* Bowl; very faint paint. Type uncertain.
> *Dimension:* Greatest diameter, 24.6 cm.
> *Provenience:* Hopi country, Arizona.

FIGURE 6: No. 21069
> *Description:* Bowl. Type uncertain.
> *Dimension:* Greatest diameter, 23.1 cm.
> *Provenience:* Hopi country, Arizona.

FIGURE 7: No. 66630
> *Description:* Ladle; handle missing.
> *Dimension:* Greatest diameter of bowl, 13 cm.
> *Provenience:* Twenty miles south of Canyon Diablo, Arizona.

FIGURE 8: No. 66648
> *Description:* Ladle; vertical loop on top of handle.
> *Dimension:* Greatest length, 17.3 cm.
> *Provenience:* Three and one-half miles east of Oraibi, Arizona.

FIGURE 9: No. 74712
> *Description:* Scoop; very thin pottery. Exterior design similar to interior.
> *Dimension:* Greatest length, 15 cm.
> *Provenience:* Bidahochi, Arizona.

FIGURE 10: No. 82019
> *Description:* Ladle; end of handle missing.
> *Dimension:* Greatest diameter of bowl, 8.5 cm.
> *Provenience:* Little Colorado Valley, probably below Winslow, Arizona.

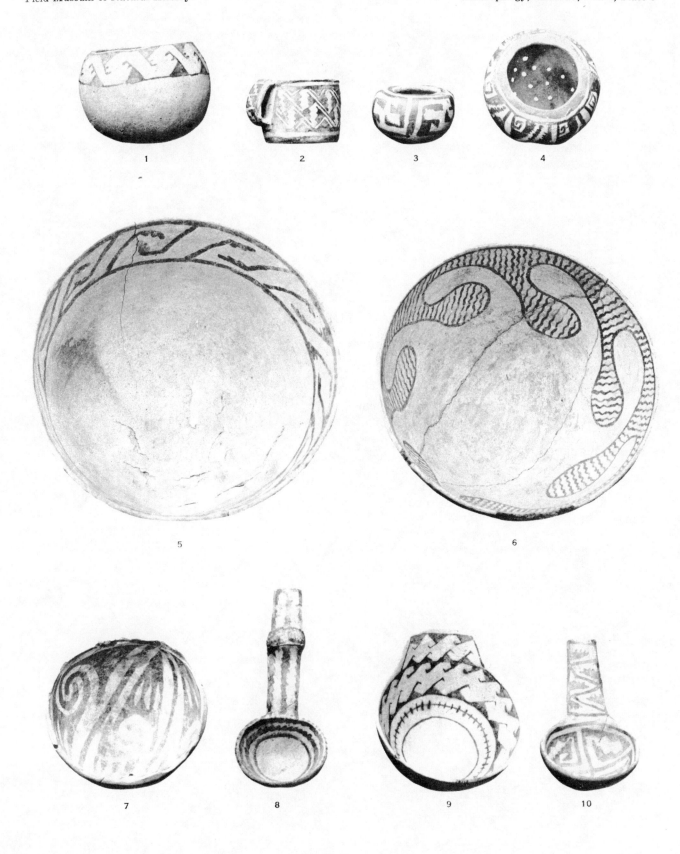

1

2

3

4

5

6

7

8

9

10

PLATE 9: BLACK MESA BLACK-ON-WHITE

Kayenta Branch

FIGURE 1: No. 21791
    Description: Large olla.
    Dimension: Greatest height, 45.7 cm.
    Provenience: Hopi country, Arizona.

FIGURE 2: No. 66658
    Description: Large olla.
    Dimension: Greatest height, 49.9 cm.
    Provenience: Oraibi, Arizona.

1

2

PLATE 10: TUSAYAN BLACK-ON-WHITE

Kayenta Branch

FIGURE 1: No. 111617

Description: Canteen; one handle missing. Concave base.
Dimension: Greatest height, 15.7 cm.
Provenience: Unknown, probably northeastern Arizona.

FIGURE 2: No. 81936

Description: Pitcher.
Dimension: Greatest height, 13.3 cm.
Provenience: Lower Little Colorado River(?), Arizona.

FIGURE 3: No. 81940

Description: Bowl; typical Tusayan design on interior, equally typical Black Mesa
design on exterior.
Dimension: Greatest diameter, 14.5 cm.
Provenience: Lower Little Colorado River(?), Arizona.

FIGURE 4: No. 72965

Description: Jar.
Dimension: Greatest diameter, 23.4 cm.
Provenience: Homolovi (No. 1), Arizona.

FIGURE 5: No. 81932

Description: Bowl. Type uncertain.
Dimension: Greatest diameter, 17.4 cm.
Provenience: Lower Little Colorado River(?), Arizona.

FIGURE 6: No. 81966

Description: Bowl; unusually graceful shape.
Dimension: Greatest diameter, 23.7 cm.
Provenience: Lower Little Colorado River(?), Arizona.

FIGURE 7: No. 81976

Description: Bowl; very deep.
Dimension: Greatest diameter, 23.5 cm.
Provenience: Lower Little Colorado River(?), Arizona.

PLATE 11: TUSAYAN BLACK-ON-WHITE
Kayenta Branch

FIGURE 1: No. 82014

    Description: Pitcher.
    Dimension: Greatest height, 11.4 cm.
    Provenience: Little Colorado Valley, probably below Winslow, Arizona.

FIGURE 2: No. 81993

    Description: Miniature pitcher.
    Dimension: Greatest height, 7.1 cm.
    Provenience: Lower Little Colorado River(?), Arizona.

FIGURE 3: No. 73950

    Description: Pitcher.
    Dimension: Greatest height, 12.6 cm.
    Provenience: San Cosmos, Arizona.

FIGURE 4: No. 81972

    Description: Ladle; hollow handle.
    Dimension: Greatest length, 27.2 cm.
    Provenience: Lower Little Colorado River(?), Arizona.

FIGURE 5: No. 81981

    Description: Ladle; note exterior decoration.
    Dimension: Greatest diameter of bowl, 9.8 cm.
    Provenience: Lower Little Colorado River(?), Arizona.

FIGURE 6: No. 81401

    Description: Ladle; white slip on coiled exterior.   Type uncertain.
    Dimension: Greatest diameter of bowl, 11.1 cm.
    Provenience: Kishuba, Arizona.

FIGURE 7: No. 66693

    Description: Ladle; unusual handle.
    Dimension: Greatest length, 25.6 cm.
    Provenience: Forty miles north of Oraibi, Arizona.

FIGURE 8: No. 81968

    Description: Bowl; very deep.
    Dimension: Greatest diameter, 23.7 cm.
    Provenience: Lower Little Colorado River(?), Arizona.

FIGURE 9: No. 82002

    Description: Bowl.
    Dimension: Greatest diameter, 25.6 cm.
    Provenience: Lower Little Colorado River(?), Arizona.

PLATE 12: TUSAYAN BLACK-ON-WHITE

Kayenta Branch

FIGURE 1: No. 81690

   Description: Pitcher. Type uncertain.
   Dimension: Height, 11 cm.
   Provenience: Twenty miles west of Allantown, Arizona (Fort Defiance 15:5). Exchange
        with Gila Pueblo.

FIGURE 2: 80777

   Description: Canteen; glossy finish. Type uncertain.
   Dimension: Height, 12.8 cm.
   Provenience: Old Walpi, Arizona.

FIGURE 3: No. 74765

   Description: Pitcher. Type uncertain.
   Dimension: Height, 9.6 cm.
   Provenience: X Ranch, Arizona.

FIGURE 4: No. 21062

   Description: Bowl. Type uncertain.
   Dimension: Greatest diameter, excluding handle, 17.6 cm.
   Provenience: Hopi country, Arizona.

FIGURE 5: No. 81516

   Description: Ladle. Type uncertain.
   Dimension: Length, 16.5 cm.
   Provenience: Chaco Canyon, New Mexico.

FIGURE 6: No. 81964

   Description: Bowl. Type uncertain.
   Dimension: Greatest diameter, 20.1 cm.
   Provenience: Lower Little Colorado River(?), Arizona.

FIGURE 7: No. 72027

   Description: Bowl. Type uncertain.
   Dimension: Greatest diameter, 24.3 cm.
   Provenience: Homolovi (No. 2), Arizona.

FIGURE 8: No. 81945

   Description: Seed jar. Type uncertain.
   Dimension: Height, 19.4 cm.
   Provenience: Lower Little Colorado River(?), Arizona.

All the above specimens are marked "Type uncertain" because they seem to be
transition pieces. Figures 1, 6, 7, and 8 show relationship with the earlier Black Mesa
Black-on-White, while Figures 2, 3, 4, and 5 foretell some of the later designs on Sagi Black-
on-White.

1

2

3

4

5

6

7

8

PLATE 13: LARGE OLLAS

Kayenta Branch

FIGURE 1: No. 75101
    Description: Tusayan Black-on-White olla.
    Dimension: Greatest height, 39.3 cm.
    Provenience: Hopi Buttes, Arizona.

FIGURE 2: No. 21111
    Description: Sagi Black-on-White olla. For main representation of this type, see
                 Plates 16–19.
    Dimension: Greatest height, 39.6 cm.
    Provenience: Hopi country, Arizona.

1

2

PLATE 14: TUSAYAN BLACK-ON-RED

Kayenta Branch

FIGURE 1: No. 81956

Description: Ladle; unslipped base and only upper surface of handle slipped.
Dimension: Greatest length, 28.9 cm.
Provenience: Lower Little Colorado River(?), Arizona.

FIGURE 2: No. 81071

Description: Bowl; unslipped base.
Dimension: Greatest diameter, 20.5 cm.
Provenience: Old Walpi, Arizona.

FIGURE 3: No. 81980

Description: Ladle; unslipped base.
Dimension: Greatest diameter of bowl, 10.7 cm.
Provenience: Lower Little Colorado River(?), Arizona.

FIGURE 4: No. 66772

Description: Seed jar; concave base too worn to show presence of slip.
Dimension: Greatest height, 8.3 cm.
Provenience: Oraibi, Arizona.

FIGURE 5: No. 66781

Description: Colander; unslipped base.
Dimension: Greatest diameter, 14.1 cm.
Provenience: Four miles west of Oraibi, Arizona.

FIGURE 6: No. 80953

Description: Canteen; two lug handles perforated vertically.
Dimension: Greatest height, 14.3 cm.
Provenience: Old Walpi, Arizona.

FIGURE 7: No. 81532

Description: Bowl; unslipped base.
Dimension: Greatest diameter, 23.3 cm.
Provenience: Chaco Canyon, New Mexico.

PLATE 15: EARLY POLYCHROMES
Kayenta Branch

FIGURE 1: No. 81989

Description: Bowl; Tusayan Polychrome. Wide red stripe on exterior. Horizontal loop handle.
Dimension: Greatest diameter, excluding handle, 15.5 cm.
Provenience: Lower Little Colorado River(?), Arizona.

FIGURE 2: No. 81995

Description: Bowl; Tusayan Polychrome. Red slip on exterior extends 11 cm. below rim.
Dimension: Greatest diameter, 21.1 cm.
Provenience: Lower Little Colorado River(?), Arizona.

FIGURE 3: No. 81385

Description: Bowl; Kayenta Polychrome. Very faint white outlines on interior, wide stripe of red slip on exterior, just below rim. Horizontal loop handle.
Dimension: Greatest diameter, excluding handle, 16.9 cm.
Provenience: Kishuba, Arizona.

FIGURE 4: No. 74733

Description: Mug; Kiet Siel Polychrome. Slip covers base.
Dimension: Greatest height, 8.6 cm.
Provenience: X Ranch, Arizona.

FIGURE 5: No. 81330

Description: Bowl; Kayenta Polychrome. White outlines for interior design, wide band of red slip on exterior.
Dimension: Greatest diameter, excluding handle, 26.7 cm.
Provenience: Kishuba, Arizona.

FIGURE 6: No. 81325

Description: Mug; Kiet Siel Polychrome. Red slip terminates with black design.
Dimension: Greatest height, 8.3 cm.
Provenience: Kishuba, Arizona.

FIGURE 7: No. 66754

Description: Bowl; Tusayan Polychrome. Base unslipped.
Dimension: Greatest diameter, excluding handle, 14.8 cm.
Provenience: Blue Canyon, Arizona.

FIGURE 8: No. 81420

Description: Jar; Kiet Siel Polychrome. Base unslipped.
Dimension: Greatest height, 17.6 cm.
Provenience: Oraibi Wash, Arizona.

FIGURE 9: No. 75133

Description: Bowl; Kiet Siel Polychrome. Base unslipped.
Dimension: Greatest diameter, 17.3 cm.
Provenience: Mesa Redonda, Arizona.

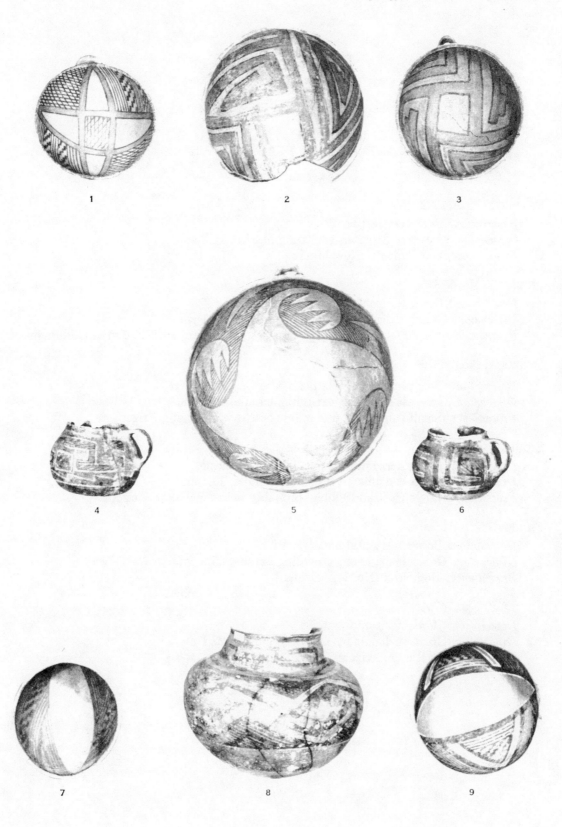

PLATE 16: SAGI BLACK-ON-WHITE
Kayenta Branch

FIGURE 1: No. 74522

> *Description:* Bowl; vertical handle.
> *Dimension:* Greatest diameter, excluding handle, 14.2 cm.
> *Provenience:* Ojo Caliente, New Mexico.

FIGURE 2: No. 81845

> *Description:* Bowl; horizontal handle.
> *Dimension:* Greatest diameter, excluding handle, 15.1 cm.
> *Provenience:* Near Flagstaff, Arizona (San Francisco Mts., 16:3).   Gift of Gila Pueblo.

FIGURE 3: No. 66626

> *Description:* Bowl; horizontal handle.
> *Dimension:* Greatest diameter, excluding handle, 17.8 cm.
> *Provenience:* Small ruin about five miles southeast of Oraibi, Arizona.

FIGURE 4: No. 82004

> *Description:* Bowl; horizontal handle.   Unusual shape.
> *Dimension:* Greatest diameter, excluding handle, 17.1 cm.
> *Provenience:* Little Colorado Valley, probably below Winslow, Arizona.

FIGURE 5: No. 72500

> *Description:* Bowl; horizontal handle.
> *Dimension:* Greatest diameter, excluding handle, 25.6 cm.
> *Provenience:* Homolovi (No. 1), Arizona.

FIGURE 6: No. 74791

> *Description:* Bowl; horizontal handle.
> *Dimension:* Greatest diameter, excluding handle, 22.1 cm.
> *Provenience:* X Ranch, Arizona.

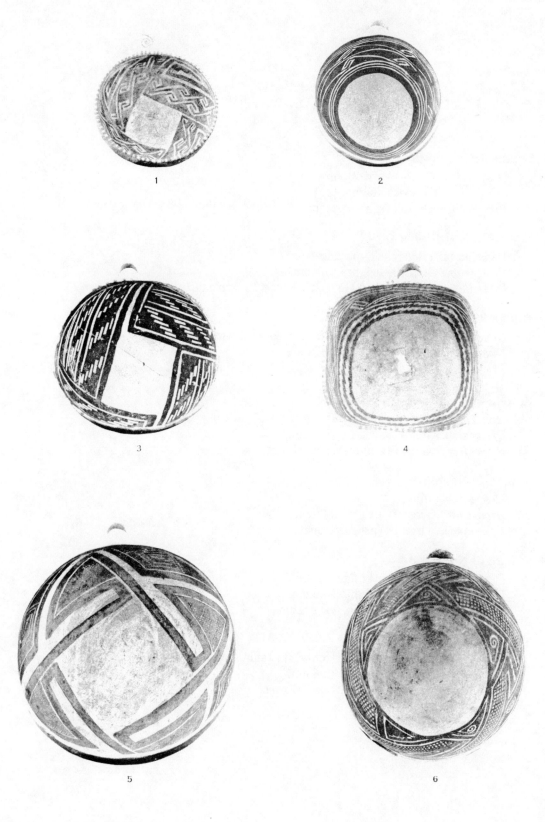

PLATE 17: SAGI BLACK-ON-WHITE

Kayenta Branch

FIGURE 1: No. 81342

    Description: Canteen; two loop handles.
    Dimension: Greatest height, 16.0 cm.
    Provenience: Oraibi Wash, Arizona.

FIGURE 2: No. 81946

    Description: Pitcher. Type uncertain.
    Dimension: Greatest height, 18.1 cm.
    Provenience: Lower Little Colorado River(?), Arizona.

FIGURE 3: No. 81304

    Description: Mug; four knobs, each decorated with spirals.
    Dimension: Greatest height, 11.7 cm.
    Provenience: Kishuba, Arizona.

FIGURE 4: No. 81538

    Description: Seed jar; very flat top.
    Dimension: Greatest height, 16.5 cm.
    Provenience: Chaco Canyon, New Mexico.

FIGURE 5: No. 81370

    Description: Mug.
    Dimension: Greatest height, 9.9 cm.
    Provenience: Oraibi Wash, Arizona.

FIGURE 6: No. 72949

    Description: Jar; slightly flaring neck.
    Dimension: Greatest height, 16.6 cm.
    Provenience: Homolovi (No. 1), Arizona.

FIGURE 7: No. 81826

    Description: Jar; unusual horizontal flattening of shoulder.
    Dimension: Greatest height, 15.6 cm.
    Provenience: Chaco Canyon, New Mexico.

PLATE 18: SAGI BLACK-ON-WHITE

Kayenta Branch

FIGURE 1: No. 74440
  Description: Bowl.
  Dimension: Greatest diameter, 20.2 cm.
  Provenience: Ojo Caliente, New Mexico.

FIGURE 2: No. 81931
  Description: Bowl.
  Dimension: Greatest diameter, 20.5 cm.
  Provenience: Lower Little Colorado River(?), Arizona.

FIGURE 3: No. 81925
  Description: Bowl.
  Dimension: Greatest diameter, 24.3 cm.
  Provenience: Lower Little Colorado River(?), Arizona.

FIGURE 4: No. 82033
  Description: Bowl; flared rim.
  Dimension: Greatest diameter, 24.1 cm.
  Provenience: Little Colorado Valley, probably below Winslow, Arizona.

FIGURE 5: No. 74792
  Description: Bowl.
  Dimension: Greatest diameter, 26.7 cm.
  Provenience: X Ranch, Arizona.

FIGURE 6: No. 81531
  Description: Bowl. Type uncertain.
  Dimension: Greatest diameter, 25.6 cm.
  Provenience: Chaco Canyon, New Mexico.

PLATE 19: SAGI BLACK-ON-WHITE
Kayenta Branch

FIGURE 1: No. 73471

    Description: Large cup; plain interior.   Type uncertain.
    Dimension: Greatest height, 9.9 cm.
    Provenience: Homolovi (No. 1), Arizona.

FIGURE 2: No. 80771

    Description: Eccentrically shaped vessel; hollow, with circular opening on flat upper
        side; two loop handles on bottom.
    Dimension: Greatest length, 29.7 cm.
    Provenience: Old Walpi, Arizona.

FIGURE 3: No. 66684

    Description: Tiny pitcher.
    Dimension: Greatest height, 9.5 cm.
    Provenience: Hopi country, Arizona.

FIGURE 4: No. 81305

    Description: Miniature ladle.
    Dimension: Greatest bowl diameter, 6.8 cm.
    Provenience: Kishuba, Arizona.

FIGURE 5: No. 81382

    Description: Ladle.
    Dimension: Greatest bowl diameter, 13.6 cm.
    Provenience: Kishuba, Arizona.

FIGURE 6: No. 81309

    Description: Ladle.
    Dimension: Greatest length, 13.1 cm.
    Provenience: Kishuba, Arizona.

FIGURE 7: No. 74767

    Description: Miniature tri-lobed pitcher.
    Dimension: Greatest height, 6.6 cm.
    Provenience: X Ranch, Arizona.

FIGURE 8: No. 44217

    Description: Ladle made from sherd (cf. design, Plate 18, Fig. 6).   Type uncertain.
    Dimension: Greatest width of bowl, 13.3 cm.
    Provenience: Hopi country, Arizona.

FIGURE 9: No. 73434

    Description: Bowl of unusual shape.   Black Mesa Black-on-White design on exterior.
        Type uncertain.
    Dimension: Greatest diameter, 19.3 cm.
    Provenience: Homolovi (No. 1), Arizona.

FIGURE 10: No. 21054

    Description: Ladle.
    Dimension: Greatest length, 18 cm.
    Provenience: Hopi country, Arizona.

PLATE 20: BIDAHOCHI BLACK-ON-WHITE
Kayenta Branch

FIGURE 1: No. 72944

Description: Jar; very flat shoulder.
Dimension: Greatest height, 11.5 cm.
Provenience: Homolovi (No. 1), Arizona.

FIGURE 2: No. 72956

Description: Jar; four corners.
Dimension: Greatest height, 13.2 cm.
Provenience: Homolovi (No. 1), Arizona.

FIGURE 3: No. 72878

Description: Pitcher.
Dimension: Greatest height, 10.4 cm.
Provenience: Homolovi (No. 1), Arizona.

FIGURE 4: No. 72955

Description: Jar.
Dimension: Greatest height, 12 cm.
Provenience: Homolovi (No. 1), Arizona.

FIGURE 5: No. 72875

Description: Mug; handle missing.
Dimension: Greatest height, 9 cm.
Provenience: Homolovi (No. 1), Arizona.

FIGURE 6: No. 72958

Description: Jar.
Dimension: Greatest height, 12.3 cm.
Provenience: Homolovi (No. 1), Arizona.

FIGURE 7: No. 72939

Description: Jar.
Dimension: Greatest height, 11.9 cm.
Provenience: Homolovi (No. 1), Arizona.

FIGURE 8: No. 74673

Description: Mug.
Dimension: Greatest height, 8.7 cm.
Provenience: Bidahochi, Arizona.

FIGURE 9: No. 72942

Description: Jar.
Dimension: Greatest height, 11.9 cm.
Provenience: Homolovi (No. 1), Arizona.

PLATE 21: BIDAHOCHI BLACK-ON-WHITE
Kayenta Branch

FIGURE 1: No. 72941
Description: Jar.
Dimension: Greatest height, 12.2 cm.
Provenience: Homolovi (No. 1), Arizona.

FIGURE 2: No. 72952
Description: Jar.
Dimension: Greatest height, 11.5 cm.
Provenience: Homolovi (No. 1), Arizona.

FIGURE 3: No. 72943
Description: Jar.   Type uncertain.
Dimension: Greatest height, 14.9 cm.
Provenience: Homolovi (No. 1), Arizona.

FIGURE 4: No. 72948
Description: Jar.
Dimension: Greatest height, 14.8 cm.
Provenience: Homolovi (No. 1), Arizona.

FIGURE 5: No. 72947
Description: Jar.
Dimension: Greatest height, 15.8 cm.
Provenience: Homolovi (No. 1), Arizona.

FIGURE 6: No. 72954
Description: Jar; rich brown paint.
Dimension: Greatest height, 14.5 cm.
Provenience: Homolovi (No. 1), Arizona.

1

2

3

4

5

6

PLATE 22: BIDAHOCHI BLACK-ON-WHITE
Kayenta Branch

FIGURE 1: No. 72748
> *Description:* Bowl.
> *Dimension:* Greatest diameter, 19.9 cm.
> *Provenience:* Homolovi (No. 1), Arizona.

FIGURE 2: No. 72482
> *Description:* Bowl.
> *Dimension:* Greatest diameter, 15.6 cm.
> *Provenience:* Homolovi (No. 1), Arizona.

FIGURE 3: No. 72706
> *Description:* Bowl.
> *Dimension:* Greatest diameter, 18.2 cm.
> *Provenience:* Homolovi (No. 1), Arizona.

FIGURE 4: No. 72452
> *Description:* Bowl; unusual exterior design.
> *Dimension:* Greatest diameter, 22.1 cm.
> *Provenience:* Homolovi (No. 1), Arizona.

FIGURE 5: No. 74775
> *Description:* Bowl. Type uncertain.
> *Dimension:* Greatest diameter, 13.7 cm.
> *Provenience:* X Ranch, Arizona.

FIGURE 6: No. 72184
> *Description:* Bowl.
> *Dimension:* Greatest diameter, 24.6 cm.
> *Provenience:* Homolovi (No. 1), Arizona.

FIGURE 7: No. 72593
> *Description:* Bowl; warped.
> *Dimension:* Greatest diameter, 22.2 cm.
> *Provenience:* Homolovi (No. 1), Arizona.

FIGURE 8: No. 72172
> *Description:* Bowl.
> *Dimension:* Greatest diameter, 14.8 cm.
> *Provenience:* Homolovi (No. 1), Arizona.

FIGURE 9: No. 72677
> *Description:* Bowl.
> *Dimension:* Greatest diameter, 24.1 cm.
> *Provenience:* Homolovi (No. 1), Arizona.

1   2   3

4   5   6

7   8   9

PLATE 23: BIDAHOCHI BLACK-ON-WHITE
Kayenta Branch

FIGURE 1: No. 72679

Description: Incurved bowl; plain, polished interior.
Dimension: Greatest diameter, 12 cm.
Provenience: Homolovi (No. 1), Arizona.

FIGURE 2: No. 72966

Description: Seed jar; reddish-brown paint.
Dimension: Greatest height, 10.7 cm.
Provenience: Homolovi (No. 1), Arizona.

FIGURE 3: No. 72881

Description: Cup; flat-bottomed.
Dimension: Greatest height, 5 cm.
Provenience: Homolovi (No. 1), Arizona.

FIGURE 4: No. 72397

Description: Ladle.
Dimension: Greatest diameter of bowl, 11.5 cm.
Provenience: Homolovi (No. 1), Arizona.

FIGURE 5: No. 81422

Description: Ladle.
Dimension: Greatest length, 24.3 cm.
Provenience: Oraibi Wash, Arizona.

FIGURE 6: No. 72401

Description: Ladle; handle perforated horizontally.
Dimension: Greatest length, 17 cm.
Provenience: Homolovi (No. 1), Arizona.

FIGURE 7: No. 73435

Description: Ladle.
Dimension: Greatest diameter of bowl, 12.3 cm.
Provenience: Homolovi (No. 1), Arizona.

FIGURE 8: No. 74710

Description: Cup; vertical loop handle missing.   Exterior design.
Dimension: Greatest diameter of bowl, 12.5 cm.
Provenience: Bidahochi, Arizona.

FIGURE 9: No. 72802

Description: Cup; vertical loop handle.
Dimension: Greatest diameter of bowl, 15.1 cm.
Provenience: Homolovi (No. 1), Arizona.

FIGURE 10: No. 72885

Description: Cup; vertical loop handle.
Dimension: Greatest diameter of bowl, 9.8 cm.
Provenience: Homolovi (No. 1), Arizona.

PLATE 24: JEDDITO BLACK-ON-ORANGE

Kayenta Branch

FIGURE 1: No. 73039
> *Description:* Jar.
> *Dimension:* Greatest height, 12.7 cm.
> *Provenience:* Homolovi (No. 1), Arizona.

FIGURE 2: No. 73043
> *Description:* Jar.
> *Dimension:* Greatest height, 13.6 cm.
> *Provenience:* Homolovi (No. 1), Arizona.

FIGURE 3: No. 73045
> *Description:* Jar (cf. design with Tusayan Black-on-White, Plate 10, Fig. 4).
> *Dimension:* Greatest height, 14.3 cm.
> *Provenience:* Homolovi (No. 1), Arizona.

FIGURE 4: No. 73024
> *Description:* Jar.
> *Dimension:* Greatest height, 14.4 cm.
> *Provenience:* Homolovi (No. 1), Arizona.

FIGURE 5: No. 73017
> *Description:* Jar.
> *Dimension:* Greatest height, 15.9 cm.
> *Provenience:* Homolovi (No. 1), Arizona.

FIGURE 6: No. 73044
> *Description:* Jar.
> *Dimension:* Greatest height, 16.3 cm.
> *Provenience:* Homolovi (No. 1), Arizona.

1

2

3

4

5

6

PLATE 25: JEDDITO BLACK-ON-ORANGE

Kayenta Branch

FIGURE 1: No. 72212

Description: Bowl; running broad line design on exterior.
Dimension: Greatest diameter, 23.1 cm.
Provenience: Homolovi (No. 1), Arizona.

FIGURE 2: No. 72652

Description: Bowl.
Dimension: Greatest diameter, 24.2 cm.
Provenience: Homolovi (No. 1), Arizona.

FIGURE 3: No. 72559

Description: Bowl.
Dimension: Greatest diameter, 25.6 cm.
Provenience: Homolovi (No. 1), Arizona.

FIGURE 4: No. 72594

Description: Bowl.
Dimension: Greatest diameter, 26.2 cm.
Provenience: Homolovi (No. 1), Arizona.

FIGURE 5: No. 72433

Description: Bowl.
Dimension: Greatest diameter, 26 cm.
Provenience: Homolovi (No. 1), Arizona.

FIGURE 6: No. 72479

Description: Bowl; single unit of opposed solid and hatched triangles on exterior
(not shown).
Dimension: Greatest diameter, 28.4 cm.
Provenience: Homolovi (No. 1), Arizona.

PLATE 26: JEDDITO BLACK-ON-ORANGE

Kayenta Branch

FIGURE 1: No. 72718
> *Description:* Bowl; six broad diagonal stripes on exterior.
> *Dimension:* Greatest diameter, 23.9 cm.
> *Provenience:* Homolovi (No. 1), Arizona.

FIGURE 2: No. 72521
> *Description:* Bowl.
> *Dimension:* Greatest diameter, 23.2 cm.
> *Provenience:* Homolovi (No. 1), Arizona.

FIGURE 3: No. 72183
> *Description:* Bowl; two broken lifelines on interior.
> *Dimension:* Greatest diameter, 20.5 cm.
> *Provenience:* Homolovi (No. 1), Arizona.

FIGURE 4: No. 75616
> *Description:* Bowl. Note beveled, ticked rim.
> *Dimension:* Greatest diameter, 15.4 cm.
> *Provenience:* Mishongnovi, Arizona.

FIGURE 5: No. 72150
> *Description:* Bowl; two broken lifelines.
> *Dimension:* Greatest diameter, 19 cm.
> *Provenience:* Homolovi (No. 1), Arizona.

FIGURE 6: No. 72715
> *Description:* Bowl.
> *Dimension:* Greatest diameter, 23.1 cm.
> *Provenience:* Homolovi (No. 1), Arizona.

FIGURE 7: No. 72511
> *Description:* Bowl.
> *Dimension:* Greatest diameter, 24.3 cm.
> *Provenience:* Homolovi (No. 1), Arizona.

PLATE 27: JEDDITO BLACK-ON-ORANGE

Kayenta Branch

FIGURE 1: No. 73078
> *Description:* Jar.
> *Dimension:* Greatest height, 14 cm.
> *Provenience:* Homolovi (No. 1), Arizona.

FIGURE 2: No. 73071
> *Description:* Jar.
> *Dimension:* Greatest height, 12.2 cm.
> *Provenience:* Homolovi (No. 1), Arizona.

FIGURE 3: No. 73018
> *Description:* Jar.
> *Dimension:* Greatest height, 14.8 cm.
> *Provenience:* Homolovi (No. 1), Arizona.

FIGURE 4: No. 74663
> *Description:* Jar.
> *Dimension:* Greatest height, 15.2 cm.
> *Provenience:* Bidahochi, Arizona.

FIGURE 5: No. 73046
> *Description:* Jar.
> *Dimension:* Greatest height, 16.8 cm.
> *Provenience:* Homolovi (No. 1), Arizona.

FIGURE 6: No. 73080
> *Description:* Jar.
> *Dimension:* Greatest height, 15.3 cm.
> *Provenience:* Homolovi (No. 1), Arizona.

1

2

3

4

5

6

PLATE 28: JEDDITO BLACK-ON-ORANGE

Kayenta Branch

FIGURE 1: No. 72796

> *Description:* Pitcher; small, with effigy handle.
> *Dimension:* Greatest height, including handle, 9.8 cm.
> *Provenience:* Homolovi (No. 1), Arizona.

FIGURE 2: No. 74658

> *Description:* Seed jar.
> *Dimension:* Greatest height, 8.6 cm.
> *Provenience:* Bidahochi, Arizona.

FIGURE 3: No. 72563

> *Description:* Turkey effigy; decorated on top surface.
> *Dimension:* Greatest length, from breast to tail, 14.1 cm.
> *Provenience:* Homolovi (No. 1), Arizona.

FIGURE 4: No. 72806

> *Description:* Cup; no exterior decoration.
> *Dimension:* Greatest diameter of bowl, excluding handle, 14.2 cm.
> *Provenience:* Homolovi (No. 1), Arizona.

FIGURE 5: No. 72427

> *Description:* Ladle.
> *Dimension:* Greatest diameter of bowl, 13.2 cm.
> *Provenience:* Homolovi (No. 1), Arizona.

FIGURE 6: No. 72365

> *Description:* Ladle.
> *Dimension:* Greatest diameter of bowl, 13.1 cm.
> *Provenience:* Homolovi (No. 1), Arizona.

FIGURE 7: No. 72798

> *Description:* Cup; no interior decoration.
> *Dimension:* Greatest diameter of bowl, excluding handle, 14 cm.
> *Provenience:* Homolovi (No. 1), Arizona.

FIGURE 8: No. 72784

> *Description:* Mug.
> *Dimension:* Greatest height, 6.3 cm.
> *Provenience:* Homolovi (No. 1), Arizona.

FIGURE 9: No. 72851

> *Description:* Pitcher, small.
> *Dimension:* Greatest height, 9 cm.
> *Provenience:* Homolovi (No. 1), Arizona.

FIGURE 10: No. 74703

> *Description:* Pitcher; small.
> *Dimension:* Greatest height, 10.2 cm.
> *Provenience:* Bidahochi, Arizona.

FIGURE 11: No. 72897

> *Description:* Mug. Note Tusayan type of design.
> *Dimension:* Greatest height, 7 cm.
> *Provenience:* Homolovi (No. 1), Arizona.

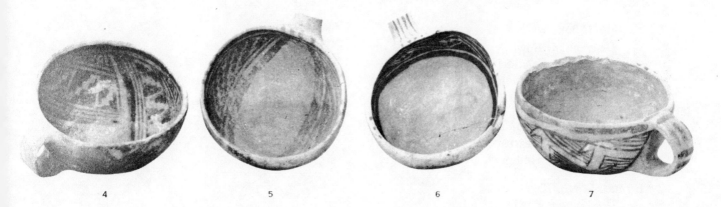

PLATE 29: JEDDITO BLACK-ON-ORANGE

Kayenta Branch

FIGURE 1: No. 72251

    Description: Bowl.
    Dimension: Greatest diameter, 18.8 cm.
    Provenience: Homolovi (No. 1), Arizona.

FIGURE 2: No. 72282

    Description: Bowl.
    Dimension: Greatest diameter, 17.3 cm.
    Provenience: Homolovi (No. 1), Arizona.

FIGURE 3: No. 72671

    Description: Bowl.
    Dimension: Greatest diameter, 18.8 cm.
    Provenience: Homolovi (No. 1), Arizona.

FIGURE 4: No. 72263

    Description: Large jar; neck missing.
    Dimension: Greatest height, 19 cm.
    Provenience: Homolovi (No. 1), Arizona.

FIGURE 5: No. 72633

    Description: Bowl.
    Dimension: Greatest diameter, 22.6 cm.
    Provenience: Homolovi (No. 1), Arizona.

FIGURE 6: No. 73027

    Description: Jar; unusual shape.
    Dimension: Greatest height, 12.9 cm.
    Provenience: Homolovi (No. 1), Arizona.

FIGURE 7: No. 72182

    Description: Bowl; simple exterior design of terraces.
    Dimension: Greatest diameter, 21.7 cm.
    Provenience: Homolovi (No. 1), Arizona.

PLATE 30: JEDDITO BLACK-ON-YELLOW

Kayenta Branch

FIGURE 1: No. 72064
>*Description:* Jar; very large.
>*Dimension:* Greatest height, 27.7 cm.
>*Provenience:* Homolovi (No. 2), Arizona.

FIGURE 2: No. 73547
>*Description:* Jar; very large.
>*Dimension:* Greatest height, 24.2 cm.
>*Provenience:* Homolovi (No. 2), Arizona.

FIGURE 3: No. 72261
>*Description:* Jar; very large.
>*Dimension:* Greatest height, 26 cm.
>*Provenience:* Homolovi (No. 1), Arizona.

FIGURE 4: No. 21201
>*Description:* Jar; very large.
>*Dimension:* Greatest height, 28.7 cm.
>*Provenience:* Hopi country, Arizona.

PLATE 31: JEDDITO BLACK-ON-YELLOW

Kayenta Branch

FIGURE 1: No. 73538

Description: Bowl.
Dimension: Greatest diameter, 21.4 cm.
Provenience: Homolovi (No. 2), Arizona.

FIGURE 2: No. 80844

Description: Jar.
Dimension: Greatest height, 13.5 cm.
Provenience: Old Walpi, Arizona.

FIGURE 3: No. 81189

Description: Bowl.
Dimension: Greatest diameter, 20.6 cm.
Provenience: Old Walpi, Arizona.

FIGURE 4: No. 73124

Description: Jar.
Dimension: Greatest height, 10.2 cm.
Provenience: Homolovi (No. 1), Arizona.

FIGURE 5: No. 72516

Description: Bowl.
Dimension: Greatest diameter, 22.2 cm.
Provenience: Homolovi (No. 1), Arizona.

FIGURE 6: No. 73057

Description: Jar.
Dimension: Greatest height, 11.9 cm.
Provenience: Homolovi (No. 1), Arizona.

FIGURE 7: No. 75559

Description: Bowl.
Dimension: Greatest diameter, 21.1 cm.
Provenience: Mishongnovi, Arizona.

FIGURE 8: No. 80686

Description: Jar.
Dimension: Greatest height, 9.9 cm.
Provenience: Old Walpi, Arizona.

FIGURE 9: No. 72524

Description: Bowl.
Dimension: Greatest diameter, 21.1 cm.
Provenience: Homolovi (No. 1), Arizona.

Figs. 1–3 show use of spirals, Figs. 4–6 triangles with hooks, and Figs. 7–9 claw design.

PLATE 32: JEDDITO BLACK-ON-YELLOW
Kayenta Branch

FIGURE 1: No. 74631
> *Description:* Bowl.
> *Dimension:* Greatest diameter, 23.5 cm.
> *Provenience:* Bidahochi, Arizona.

FIGURE 2: No. 80647
> *Description:* Jar.
> *Dimension:* Greatest height, 12.8 cm.
> *Provenience:* Old Walpi, Arizona.

FIGURE 3: No. 72661
> *Description:* Bowl.
> *Dimension:* Greatest diameter, 21.8 cm.
> *Provenience:* Homolovi (No. 1), Arizona.

FIGURE 4: No. 74687
> *Description:* Mug.
> *Dimension:* Greatest height, 7.9 cm.
> *Provenience:* Bidahochi, Arizona.

FIGURE 5: No. 80779
> *Description:* Bowl.
> *Dimension:* Greatest diameter, 20.7 cm.
> *Provenience:* Mishongnovi, Arizona.

FIGURE 6: No. 74692
> *Description:* Mug.
> *Dimension:* Greatest height, 8.1 cm.
> *Provenience:* Bidahochi, Arizona.

FIGURE 7: No. 72028
> *Description:* Bowl.
> *Dimension:* Greatest diameter, 21.8 cm.
> *Provenience:* Homolovi (No. 2), Arizona.

FIGURE 8: No. 52763
> *Description:* Jar.
> *Dimension:* Greatest height, 12.9 cm.
> *Provenience:* Homolovi (No. 2), Arizona.

FIGURE 9: No. 72042
> *Description:* Bowl.
> *Dimension:* Greatest diameter, 22.3 cm.
> *Provenience:* Homolovi (No. 2), Arizona.

Figs. 1–3 show use of large amounts of hachure, Figs. 4–6 ticked elements, and Figs. 7–9 smaller amounts of hachure as integral parts of the whole design.

PLATE 33: JEDDITO BLACK-ON-YELLOW

Kayenta Branch

FIGURE 1: No. 73575

Description: Bowl.
Dimension: Greatest diameter, 22.9 cm.
Provenience: Homolovi (No. 2), Arizona.

FIGURE 2: No. 75524

Description: Pitcher.
Dimension: Greatest height, 12.3 cm.
Provenience: Mishongnovi, Arizona.

FIGURE 3: No. 73577

Description: Bowl.
Dimension: Greatest diameter, 20.6 cm.
Provenience: Homolovi (No. 2), Arizona.

FIGURE 4: No. 73097

Description: Jar.
Dimension: Greatest height, 9.1 cm.
Provenience: Homolovi (No. 1), Arizona.

FIGURE 5: No. 72153

Description: Bowl.
Dimension: Greatest diameter, 25.4 cm.
Provenience: Homolovi (No. 1), Arizona.

FIGURE 6: No. 72779

Description: Mug; handle missing.
Dimension: Greatest height, 9 cm.
Provenience: Homolovi (No. 1), Arizona.

FIGURE 7: No. 72589

Description: Bowl.
Dimension: Greatest diameter, 21.5 cm.
Provenience: Homolovi (No. 1), Arizona.

FIGURE 8: No. 75702

Description: Jar.
Dimension: Greatest height, 10.5 cm.
Provenience: Mishongnovi, Arizona.

FIGURE 9: No. 72255

Description: Bowl.
Dimension: Greatest diameter, 21.3 cm.
Provenience: Homolovi (No. 1), Arizona.

All the figures on this plate represent variations in use of terraced figure, probably the most common design in the collection of this pottery-type.

PLATE 34: JEDDITO BLACK-ON-YELLOW
Kayenta Branch

FIGURE 1: No. 75539
Description: Bowl.
Dimension: Greatest diameter, 20.8 cm.
Provenience: Mishongnovi, Arizona.

FIGURE 2: No. 73062
Description: Jar.
Dimension: Greatest height, 11.2 cm.
Provenience: Homolovi (No. 1), Arizona.

FIGURE 3: No. 72244
Description: Bowl.
Dimension: Greatest diameter, 22.7 cm.
Provenience: Homolovi (No. 1), Arizona.

FIGURE 4: No. 73065
Description: Jar.
Dimension: Greatest height, 12.7 cm.
Provenience: Homolovi (No. 1), Arizona.

FIGURE 5: No. 72018
Description: Bowl.
Dimension: Greatest diameter, 23.9 cm.
Provenience: Homolovi (No. 2), Arizona.

FIGURE 6: No. 73543
Description: Jar.
Dimension: Greatest height, 11.5 cm.
Provenience: Homolovi (No. 2), Arizona.

FIGURE 7: No. 67175
Description: Bowl.
Dimension: Greatest diameter, 22.3 cm.
Provenience: Shungopovi, Arizona.

FIGURE 8: No. 73487
Description: Mug.
Dimension: Greatest height, 10.1 cm.
Provenience: Homolovi (No. 1), Arizona.

FIGURE 9: No. 73580
Description: Bowl.
Dimension: Greatest diameter, 24.8 cm.
Provenience: Homolovi (No. 2), Arizona.

Figs. 1–3 show variations of checkerboard design, Figs. 4–6 cross-hachure and basket-weave, and Figs. 7–9 squiggly hachure.

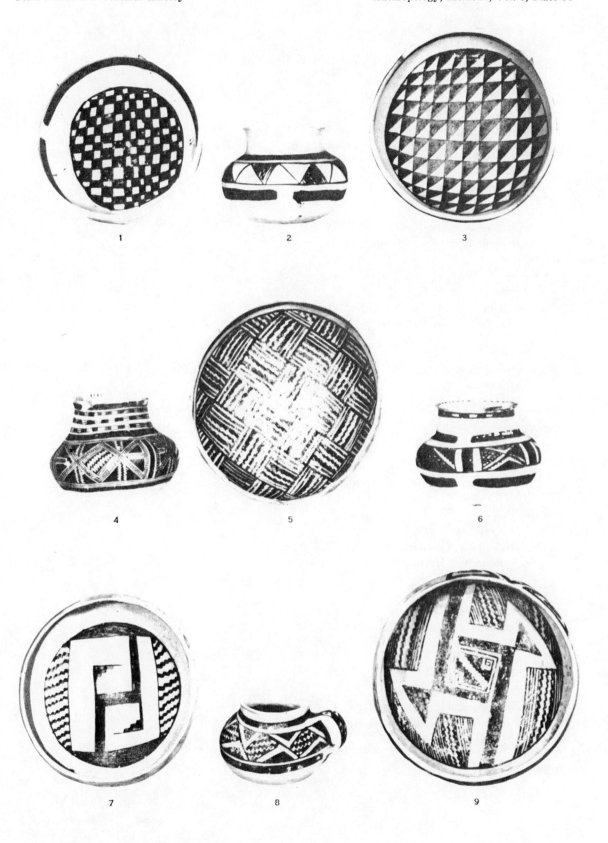

PLATE 35: JEDDITO BLACK-ON-YELLOW

Kayenta Branch

FIGURE 1: No. 52697
> *Description:* Bowl.
> *Dimension:* Greatest diameter, 20.5 cm.
> *Provenience:* Homolovi (No. 2), Arizona.

FIGURE 2: No. 75275
> *Description:* Bowl.
> *Dimension:* Greatest diameter, 16.5 cm.
> *Provenience:* Sikyatki, Arizona.

FIGURE 3: No. 75565
> *Description:* Bowl.
> *Dimension:* Greatest diameter, 20.3 cm.
> *Provenience:* Mishongnovi, Arizona.

FIGURE 4: No. 75706
> *Description:* Bowl.
> *Dimension:* Greatest diameter, 21.3 cm.
> *Provenience:* Mishongnovi, Arizona.

FIGURE 5: No. 73362
> *Description:* Bowl.
> *Dimension:* Greatest diameter, 22.1 cm.
> *Provenience:* Chevellon, Arizona.

FIGURE 6: No. 72712
> *Description:* Bowl.
> *Dimension:* Greatest diameter, 22.4 cm.
> *Provenience:* Homolovi (No. 1), Arizona.

FIGURE 7: No. 72176
> *Description:* Bowl.
> *Dimension:* Greatest diameter, 15.2 cm.
> *Provenience:* Homolovi (No. 1), Arizona.

FIGURE 8: No. 75825
> *Description:* Bowl.
> *Dimension:* Greatest diameter, 21 cm.
> *Provenience:* Mishongnovi, Arizona.

The variety of designs in this type is almost inexhaustible. Plates 35–37 illustrate a miscellany of designs.

PLATE 36: JEDDITO BLACK-ON-YELLOW

Kayenta Branch

FIGURE 1: No. 73567

> *Description:* Bowl.
> *Dimension:* Greatest diameter, 20.6 cm.
> *Provenience:* Homolovi (No. 2), Arizona.

FIGURE 2: No. 80792

> *Description:* Bowl.
> *Dimension:* Greatest diameter, 11.5 cm.
> *Provenience:* Old Walpi, Arizona.

FIGURE 3: No. 75494

> *Description:* Bowl; exterior also covered with spirals.
> *Dimension:* Greatest diameter, 18.1 cm.
> *Provenience:* Mishongnovi, Arizona.

FIGURE 4: No. 80532

> *Description:* Bowl.
> *Dimension:* Greatest diameter, 21.8 cm.
> *Provenience:* Old Walpi, Arizona.

FIGURE 5: No. 75944

> *Description:* Bowl.
> *Dimension:* Greatest diameter, 22.7 cm.
> *Provenience:* Mishongnovi, Arizona.

FIGURE 6: No. 52654

> *Description:* Bowl.
> *Dimension:* Greatest diameter, 20.7 cm.
> *Provenience:* Homolovi (No. 2), Arizona.

FIGURE 7: No. 52701

> *Description:* Bowl.
> *Dimension:* Greatest diameter, 16.5 cm.
> *Provenience:* Homolovi (No. 2), Arizona.

FIGURE 8: No. 75414

> *Description:* Bowl.
> *Dimension:* Greatest diameter, 23.6 cm.
> *Provenience:* Sikyatki, Arizona.

PLATE 37: JEDDITO BLACK-ON-YELLOW

Kayenta Branch

FIGURE 1: No. 75568
>*Description:* Bowl.
>*Dimension:* Greatest diameter, 19.8 cm.
>*Provenience:* Mishongnovi, Arizona.

FIGURE 2: No. 75286
>*Description:* Bowl.
>*Dimension:* Greatest diameter, 16.2 cm.
>*Provenience:* Sikyatki, Arizona.

FIGURE 3: No. 73513
>*Description:* Bowl.
>*Dimension:* Greatest diameter, 21.5 cm.
>*Provenience:* Homolovi (No. 2), Arizona.

FIGURE 4: No. 80030
>*Description:* Bowl.
>*Dimension:* Greatest diameter, 20.7 cm.
>*Provenience:* Chukubi (one mile northeast of Shipaulovi), Arizona.

FIGURE 5: No. 75271
>*Description:* Bowl.
>*Dimension:* Greatest diameter, 17.2 cm.
>*Provenience:* Sikyatki, Arizona.

FIGURE 6: No. 73535
>*Description:* Bowl.
>*Dimension:* Greatest diameter, 21.7 cm.
>*Provenience:* Homolovi (No. 2), Arizona.

FIGURE 7: No. 80033
>*Description:* Bowl.
>*Dimension:* Greatest diameter, 20.9 cm.
>*Provenience:* Chukubi (one mile northeast of Shipaulovi), Arizona.

FIGURE 8: No. 75823
>*Description:* Bowl.
>*Dimension:* Greatest diameter, 15.3 cm.
>*Provenience:* Mishongnovi, Arizona.

FIGURE 9: No. 52699
>*Description:* Bowl.
>*Dimension:* Greatest diameter, 21.5 cm.
>*Provenience:* Homolovi (No. 2), Arizona.

Kayenta Branch

FIGURE 1: No. 75216
> *Description:* Jar.
> *Dimension:* Greatest height, 15.7 cm.
> *Provenience:* Sikyatki, Arizona.

FIGURE 2: No. 80648
> *Description:* Jar.
> *Dimension:* Greatest height, 12.2 cm.
> *Provenience:* Old Walpi, Arizona.

FIGURE 3: No. 73056
> *Description:* Jar.
> *Dimension:* Greatest height, 13.6 cm.
> *Provenience:* Homolovi (No. 1), Arizona.

FIGURE 4: No. 73015
> *Description:* Jar.
> *Dimension:* Greatest height, 12.5 cm.
> *Provenience:* Homolovi (No. 1), Arizona.

FIGURE 5: No. 81101
> *Description:* Jar.
> *Dimension:* Greatest height, 14.7 cm.
> *Provenience:* Old Walpi, Arizona.

FIGURE 6: No. 73068
> *Description:* Jar.
> *Dimension:* Greatest height, 12.3 cm.
> *Provenience:* Homolovi (No. 1), Arizona.

FIGURE 7: No. 73069
> *Description:* Jar.
> *Dimension:* Greatest height, 12.1 cm.
> *Provenience:* Homolovi (No. 1), Arizona.

FIGURE 8: No. 67231
> *Description:* Jar.
> *Dimension:* Greatest height, 16.2 cm.
> *Provenience:* Shungopovi, Arizona.

FIGURE 9: No. 73130
> *Description:* Jar.
> *Dimension:* Greatest height, 10.3 cm.
> *Provenience:* Homolovi (No. 1), Arizona.

Figs. 2, 5, and 8 show early appearance of later Sikyatki Polychrome jar shape. The other six specimens show survival of earlier Jeddito Black-on-Orange jar shape. Mr. J. O. Brew agrees with our opinion.

1

2

3

4

5

6

7

8

9

PLATE 39: JEDDITO BLACK-ON-YELLOW

Kayenta Branch

FIGURE 1: No. 80786
  Description: Bowl; human figure painted inside.
  Dimension: Greatest diameter, 23.4 cm.
  Provenience: Old Walpi, Arizona.

FIGURE 2: No. 72318
  Description: Ladle; sculptured papoose in cradle serving as handle.
  Dimension: Greatest length, 15.5 cm.
  Provenience: Homolovi (No. 1), Arizona.

FIGURE 3: No. 80061
  Description: Bowl; three human(?) figures in interior.
  Dimension: Greatest diameter, 23.8 cm.
  Provenience: Chukubi (one mile northeast of Shipaulovi), Arizona.

FIGURE 4: No. 80806
  Description: Bowl; human(?) figure in interior.
  Dimension: Greatest diameter, 21.4 cm.
  Provenience: Old Walpi, Arizona.

FIGURE 5: No. 80898
  Description: Ladle; unpolished.
  Dimension: Greatest fragmentary length, 14.6 cm.
  Provenience: Old Walpi, Arizona.

FIGURE 6: No. 72273
  Description: Bowl; human head painted inside.
  Dimension: Greatest diameter, 22 cm.
  Provenience: Homolovi (No. 1), Arizona.

FIGURE 7: No. 66731
  Description: Bowl; human hand outlined by stippling. All six bowls in our collection
    showing hands are stippled.
  Dimension: Greatest diameter, 22.7 cm.
  Provenience: North of Oraibi, Arizona.

FIGURE 8: No. 80106
  Description: Ladle; simple geometric design on interior.
  Dimension: Greatest length, 18.2 cm.
  Provenience: Awatovi, Arizona.

FIGURE 9: No. 75503
  Description: Bowl; line drawing of crying human being.
  Dimension: Greatest diameter, 24.2 cm.
  Provenience: Mishongnovi, Arizona.

PLATE 40: JEDDITO BLACK-ON-YELLOW

Kayenta Branch

FIGURE 1: No. 72271

Description: Bowl; painting of lizard inside.
Dimension: Greatest diameter, 21.7 cm.
Provenience: Homolovi (No. 1), Arizona.

FIGURE 2: No. 67212

Description: Ladle; painting of monster.
Dimension: Greatest diameter of bowl, 9.9 cm.
Provenience: Nanapii, Arizona.

FIGURE 3: No. 75244

Description: Bowl; painting of bird(?).
Dimension: Greatest diameter, 22.5 cm.
Provenience: Sikyatki, Arizona.

FIGURE 4: No. 75781

Description: Bowl; painting of moth.
Dimension: Greatest diameter, 20.4 cm.
Provenience: Mishongnovi, Arizona.

FIGURE 5: No. 52686

Description: Mug; effigy handle.
Dimension: Greatest height, excluding handle, 9.9 cm.
Provenience: Homolovi (No. 2), Arizona.

FIGURE 6: No. 72277

Description: Bowl; painting of bird.
Dimension: Greatest diameter, 19 cm.
Provenience: Homolovi (No. 1), Arizona.

FIGURE 7: No. 21163

Description: Bowl; conventionalized design.
Dimension: Greatest diameter, 23.6 cm.
Provenience: Hopi country, Arizona.

FIGURE 8: No. 52719

Description: Bird effigy vessel.
Dimension: Greatest height, 4.9 cm.
Provenience: Homolovi (No. 2), Arizona.

FIGURE 9: No. 21186

Description: Bowl; conventionalized design.
Dimension: Greatest diameter, 23.7 cm.
Provenience: Hopi country, Arizona.

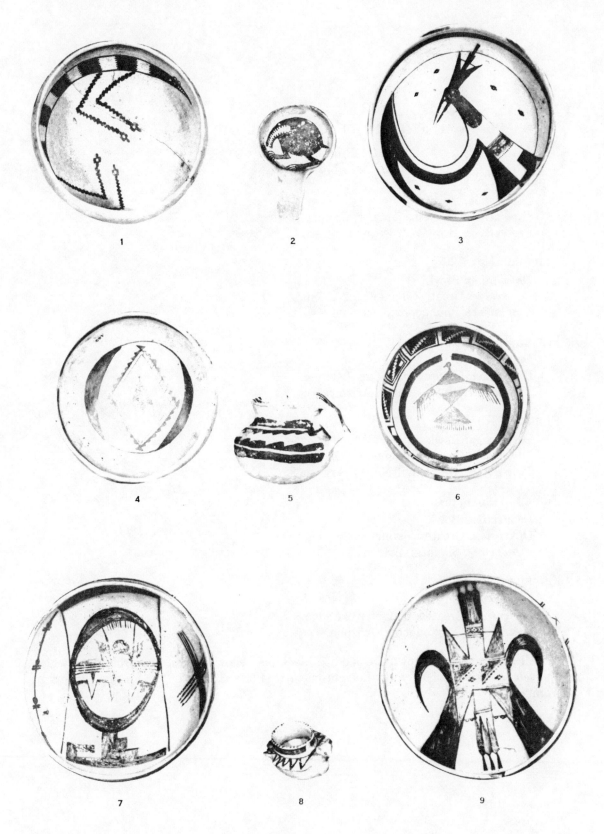

PLATE 41: JEDDITO BLACK-ON-YELLOW

Kayenta Branch

FIGURE 1: No. 21158
> *Description:* Bowl.
> *Dimension:* Greatest diameter, 26 cm.
> *Provenience:* Hopi country, Arizona.

FIGURE 2: No. 67207
> *Description:* Bowl.
> *Dimension:* Greatest diameter, 25.5 cm.
> *Provenience:* Shungopovi, Arizona.

FIGURE 3: No. 21154
> *Description:* Bowl.
> *Dimension:* Greatest diameter, 24.4 cm.
> *Provenience:* Hopi country, Arizona.

FIGURE 4: No. 72284
> *Description:* Bowl.
> *Dimension:* Greatest diameter, 22.5 cm.
> *Provenience:* Homolovi (No. 1), Arizona.

FIGURE 5: No. 67157
> *Description:* Bowl.
> *Dimension:* Greatest diameter, 25.7 cm.
> *Provenience:* Sikyatki, Arizona.

FIGURE 6: No. 75799
> *Description:* Bowl.
> *Dimension:* Greatest diameter, 24.8 cm.
> *Provenience:* Mishongnovi, Arizona.

All the bowls here shown are Jeddito Black-on-Yellow, but all have the shape which later becomes typical of Sikyatki Polychrome (see Plate 52). Mr. J. O. Brew concurs in this opinion.

PLATE 42: JEDDITO BLACK-ON-YELLOW, UNUSUAL SHAPES
Kayenta Branch

FIGURE 1: No. 72683

Description: Colander. Only one of this type in collection.
Dimension: Greatest diameter, 13.4 cm.
Provenience: Homolovi (No. 1), Arizona.

FIGURE 2: No. 81112

Description: Jar; originally had basket-handle(?).
Dimension: Greatest height, excluding handle stumps, 7.1 cm.
Provenience: Old Walpi, Arizona.

FIGURE 3: No. 75239

Description: Flat-bottomed mug. Two other similar mugs, one without handle, in collection.
Dimension: Greatest height, 4.5 cm.
Provenience: Sikyatki, Arizona.

FIGURE 4: No. 72765

Description: Incurved bowl; no interior decoration. Twelve others, in collection, with and without interior decoration.
Dimension: Greatest height, 7.2 cm.
Provenience: Homolovi (No. 1), Arizona.

FIGURE 5: No. 80989

Description: Ridged jar. Six others in collection, with variations of this treatment.
Dimension: Greatest height, 8.6 cm.
Provenience: Old Walpi, Arizona.

FIGURE 6: No. 21200

Description: Wide-mouthed jar. Seven others in collection.
Dimension: Greatest height, 10.2 cm.
Provenience: Hopi country, Arizona.

FIGURE 7: No. 80918

Description: Jar; horizontal handle. Collection includes three or four similar jars.
Dimension: Greatest height, 8.8 cm.
Provenience: Old Walpi, Arizona.

FIGURE 8: No. 80776

Description: Bowl; corrugated and painted. One jar in collection, the upper half corrugated, the lower painted.
Dimension: Greatest diameter, 12.2 cm.
Provenience: Old Walpi, Arizona.

FIGURE 9: No. 67159

Description: Bowl; square and unpolished. Two others in collection.
Dimension: Greatest height, 6.3 cm.
Provenience: Two miles south of Oraibi, Arizona.

FIGURE 10: No. 72116

Description: Ring-shaped vessel. The only one of this shape in collection.
Dimension: Greatest height, 8.1 cm.
Provenience: Homolovi (No. 2), Arizona.

FIGURE 11: No. 21192

Description: Bowl; plain interior. One other, larger, in collection.
Dimension: Greatest diameter, 12.8 cm.
Provenience: Hopi country, Arizona.

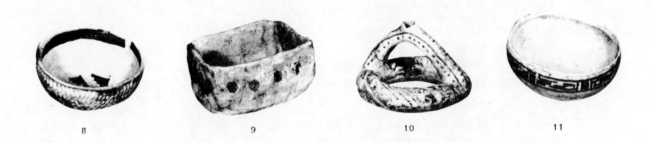

PLATE 43: JEDDITO BLACK-ON-YELLOW
Kayenta Branch

FIGURE 1: No. 21188

> *Description:* Ladle; round, pointed handle.
> *Dimension:* Greatest length, 22.2 cm.
> *Provenience:* Hopi country, Arizona.

FIGURE 2: No. 81046

> *Description:* Ladle; half-gourd type with ridge between bowl and handle.
> *Dimension:* Greatest length, 20.9 cm.
> *Provenience:* Old Walpi, Arizona.

FIGURE 3: No. 67189

> *Description:* Ladle; flat, perforated handle.
> *Dimension:* Greatest length, 26.9 cm.
> *Provenience:* Near Oraibi, Arizona.

FIGURE 4: No. 80992

> *Description:* Ladle; round, perforated handle.
> *Dimension:* Greatest length, 17.3 cm.
> *Provenience:* Old Walpi, Arizona.

FIGURE 5: No. 80229

> *Description:* Ladle; concave, effigy-head handle.
> *Dimension:* Greatest length, 18.3 cm.
> *Provenience:* Awatovi, Arizona.

FIGURE 6: No. 81050

> *Description:* Ladle; half-gourd type, perforated.
> *Dimension:* Greatest length, 18.2 cm.
> *Provenience:* Old Walpi, Arizona.

FIGURE 7: No. 80226

> *Description:* Ladle; curved round handle.
> *Dimension:* Greatest length, 13.7 cm.
> *Provenience:* Awatovi, Arizona.

FIGURE 8: No. 72338

> *Description:* Ladle; round handle, perforated horizontally.
> *Dimension:* Greatest length, 20.8 cm.
> *Provenience:* Homolovi (No. 1), Arizona.

FIGURE 9: No. 80765

> *Description:* Ladle; flat bowl with ridge dividing it from handle.
> *Dimension:* Greatest diameter of bowl, 14.5 cm.
> *Provenience:* Old Walpi, Arizona.

FIGURE 10: No. 52720

> *Description:* Ladle; loop handle.
> *Dimension:* Greatest diameter of bowl, 12.1 cm.
> *Provenience:* Homolovi (No. 2), Arizona.

FIGURE 11: No. 21160

> *Description:* Ladle; half-gourd type with flat bowl.
> *Dimension:* Greatest diameter of bowl, 15.2 cm.
> *Provenience:* Hopi country, Arizona.

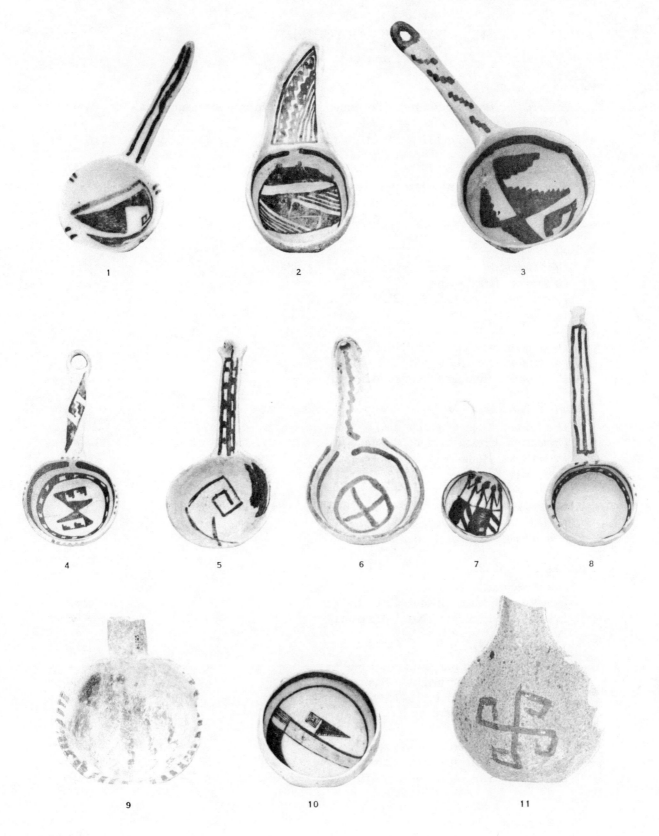

PLATE 44: BIDAHOCHI POLYCHROME
Kayenta Branch

FIGURE 1: No. 72676

> *Description:* Bowl; unusual flat-bottomed shape.   No interior decoration.
> *Dimension:* Greatest diameter, 17.1 cm.
> *Provenience:* Homolovi (No. 1), Arizona.

FIGURE 2: No. 72805

> *Description:* Ladle; no white paint on interior.
> *Dimension:* Greatest diameter, excluding handle, 14.2 cm.
> *Provenience:* Homolovi (No. 1), Arizona.

FIGURE 3: No. 72063

> *Description:* Bowl; incurved rim.
> *Dimension:* Greatest height, 7.8 cm.
> *Provenience:* Homolovi (No. 2), Arizona.

FIGURE 4: No. 72789

> *Description:* Jar; two effigy handles.
> *Dimension:* Greatest height, 12.1 cm.
> *Provenience:* Homolovi (No. 1), Arizona.

FIGURE 5: No. 72772

> *Description:* Mug; effigy handle.
> *Dimension:* Greatest height, 4.7 cm.
> *Provenience:* Homolovi (No. 1), Arizona.

FIGURE 6: No. 74684

> *Description:* Frog-effigy vessel.
> *Dimension:* Greatest length, 14 cm.
> *Provenience:* Bidahochi, Arizona.

FIGURE 7: No. 73021

> *Description:* Pitcher.
> *Dimension:* Greatest height, 12.1 cm.
> *Provenience:* Homolovi (No. 1), Arizona.

FIGURE 8: No. 72817

> *Description:* Mug; purple paint.
> *Dimension:* Greatest height, 7.8 cm.
> *Provenience:* Homolovi (No. 1), Arizona.

FIGURE 9: No. 73023

> *Description:* Pitcher.
> *Dimension:* Greatest height, 12.6 cm.
> *Provenience:* Homolovi (No. 1), Arizona.

1

2

3

4

5

6

7

8

9

PLATE 45: BIDAHOCHI POLYCHROME
Kayenta Branch

FIGURE 1: No. 72213

> *Description:* Bowl; no exterior decoration.
> *Dimension:* Greatest diameter, 22.1 cm.
> *Provenience:* Homolovi (No. 1), Arizona.

FIGURE 2: No. 72388

> *Description:* Ladle.
> *Dimension:* Greatest diameter of bowl, 10.9 cm.
> *Provenience:* Homolovi (No. 1), Arizona.

FIGURE 3: No. 72281

> *Description:* Bowl.
> *Dimension:* Greatest diameter, 17.5 cm.
> *Provenience:* Homolovi (No. 1), Arizona.

FIGURE 4: No. 72742

> *Description:* Bowl.
> *Dimension:* Greatest diameter, 21.5 cm.
> *Provenience:* Homolovi (No. 1), Arizona.

FIGURE 5: No. 72604

> *Description:* Bowl.
> *Dimension:* Greatest diameter, 20.7 cm.
> *Provenience:* Homolovi (No. 1), Arizona.

FIGURE 6: No. 72495

> *Description:* Bowl.
> *Dimension:* Greatest diameter, 21.5 cm.
> *Provenience:* Homolovi (No. 1), Arizona.

FIGURE 7: No. 72220

> *Description:* Bowl.
> *Dimension:* Greatest diameter, 21.1 cm.
> *Provenience:* Homolovi (No. 1), Arizona.

1   2   3

4   5

6   7

PLATE 46: BIDAHOCHI POLYCHROME
Kayenta Branch

FIGURE 1: No. 72753
> *Description:* Bowl.
> *Dimension:* Greatest diameter, 21.6 cm.
> *Provenience:* Homolovi (No. 1), Arizona.

FIGURE 2: No. 72761
> *Description:* Bowl.
> *Dimension:* Greatest diameter, 21.1 cm.
> *Provenience:* Homolovi (No. 1), Arizona.

FIGURE 3: No. 72221
> *Description:* Bowl.
> *Dimension:* Greatest diameter, 21.1 cm.
> *Provenience:* Homolovi (No. 1), Arizona.

FIGURE 4: No. 72758
> *Description:* Bowl.
> *Dimension:* Greatest diameter, 21.5 cm.
> *Provenience:* Homolovi (No. 1), Arizona.

FIGURE 5: No. 74625
> *Description:* Bowl; no exterior decoration.
> *Dimension:* Greatest diameter, 22.1 cm.
> *Provenience:* Bidahochi, Arizona.

FIGURE 6: No. 72168
> *Description:* Bowl.
> *Dimension:* Greatest diameter, 21.7 cm.
> *Provenience:* Homolovi (No. 1), Arizona.

1

2

3

4

5

6

PLATE 47: BIDAHOCHI POLYCHROME

Kayenta Branch

FIGURE 1: No. 73010

Description: Jar.
Dimension: Greatest height, 14 cm.
Provenience: Homolovi (No. 1), Arizona.

FIGURE 2: No. 73104

Description: Jar.
Dimension: Greatest height, 11.5 cm.
Provenience: Homolovi (No. 1), Arizona.

FIGURE 3: No. 67193

Description: Jar.
Dimension: Greatest height, 12 cm.
Provenience: Shungopovi, Arizona.

FIGURE 4: No. 80144

Description: Jar; unusual neck.
Dimension: Greatest height, 13.5 cm.
Provenience: Awatovi, Arizona.

FIGURE 5: No. 73112

Description: Jar; conventionalized bird in white on neck.
Dimension: Greatest height, 15.3 cm.
Provenience: Homolovi (No. 1), Arizona.

FIGURE 6: No. 73133

Description: Jar; paint a rich blue.
Dimension: Greatest height, 15.4 cm.
Provenience: Homolovi (No. 1), Arizona.

1

2

3

4

5

6

PLATE 48: SIKYATKI POLYCHROME

Kayenta Branch

FIGURE 1: No. 75573

Description: Bowl.
Dimension: Greatest diameter, 20.3 cm.
Provenience: Mishongnovi, Arizona.

FIGURE 2: No. 81154

Description: Jar.
Dimension: Greatest height, 9.8 cm.
Provenience: Old Walpi, Arizona.

FIGURE 3: No. 67204

Description: Bowl.
Dimension: Greatest diameter, 19.6 cm.
Provenience: Shungopovi, Arizona.

FIGURE 4: No. 75417

Description: Jar.
Dimension: Greatest height, 11.6 cm.
Provenience: Sikyatki, Arizona.

FIGURE 5: No. 80939

Description: Bowl.
Dimension: Greatest diameter, 18.8 cm.
Provenience: Old Walpi, Arizona.

FIGURE 6: No. 67209

Description: Jar.
Dimension: Greatest height, 10.8 cm.
Provenience: Shungopovi, Arizona.

FIGURE 7: No. 80058

Description: Bowl.
Dimension: Greatest diameter, 22.6 cm.
Provenience: Chukubi (one mile northwest of Shipaulovi), Arizona.

FIGURE 8: No. 80178

Description: Jar.
Dimension: Greatest height, 13.6 cm.
Provenience: Awatovi, Arizona.

FIGURE 9: No. 21189

Description: Bowl.
Dimension: Greatest diameter, 21.8 cm.
Provenience: Hopi country, Arizona.

All the above specimens retain shapes typical of antecedent Jeddito Black-on-Yellow. In Figs. 1, 2, 5, and 6, even style of design is that of earlier type. Mr. J. O. Brew agrees with this analysis.

1

2

3

4

5

6

7

8

9

PLATE 49: SIKYATKI POLYCHROME

Kayenta Branch

FIGURE 1: No. 75273

> *Description:* Bowl; unusual rim shape.
> *Dimension:* Greatest diameter, 17.7 cm.
> *Provenience:* Sikyatki, Arizona.

FIGURE 2: No. 75428

> *Description:* Bowl.
> *Dimension:* Greatest diameter, 25.9 cm.
> *Provenience:* Sikyatki, Arizona.

FIGURE 3: No. 80813

> *Description:* Bowl.
> *Dimension:* Greatest diameter, 17.9 cm.
> *Provenience:* Old Walpi, Arizona.

FIGURE 4: No. 81066

> *Description:* Bowl.
> *Dimension:* Greatest diameter, 28.4 cm.
> *Provenience:* Old Walpi, Arizona.

FIGURE 5: No. 80097

> *Description:* Bowl.
> *Dimension:* Greatest diameter, 26.7 cm.
> *Provenience:* Awatovi, Arizona.

FIGURE 6: No. 80536

> *Description:* Bowl.
> *Dimension:* Greatest diameter, 21.8 cm.
> *Provenience:* Old Walpi, Arizona.

FIGURE 7: No. 21165

> *Description:* Bowl.
> *Dimension:* Greatest diameter, 23.9 cm.
> *Provenience:* Hopi country, Arizona.

FIGURE 8: No. 80959

> *Description:* Bowl.
> *Dimension:* Greatest diameter, 21.4 cm.
> *Provenience:* Old Walpi, Arizona.

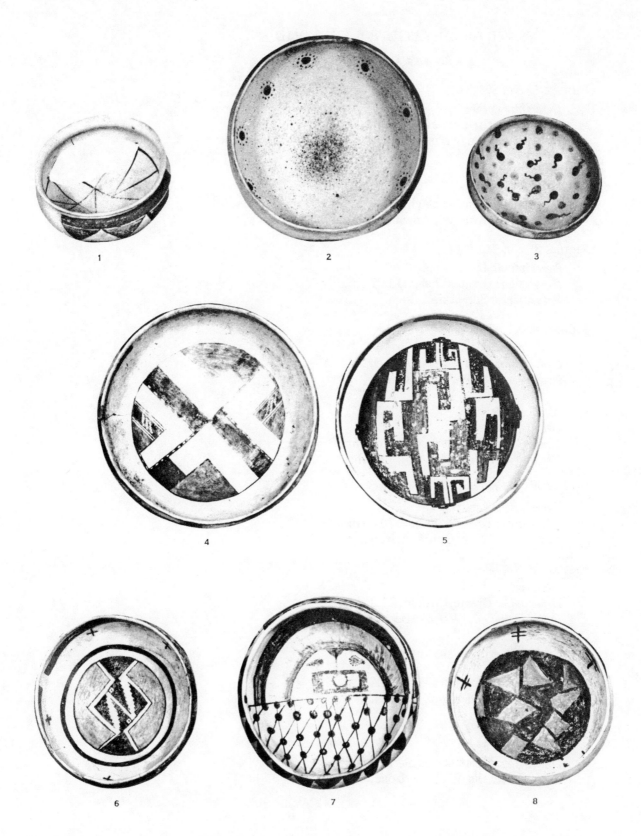

PLATE 50: SIKYATKI POLYCHROME
Kayenta Branch

FIGURE 1: No. 80842
> *Description:* Jar.
> *Dimension:* Greatest height, 13.6 cm.
> *Provenience:* Old Walpi, Arizona.

FIGURE 2: No. 80135
> *Description:* Jar.
> *Dimension:* Greatest height, 10.8 cm.
> *Provenience:* Awatovi, Arizona.

FIGURE 3: No. 75217
> *Description:* Jar.
> *Dimension:* Greatest height, 11.7 cm.
> *Provenience:* Sikyatki, Arizona.

FIGURE 4: No. 80856
> *Description:* Jar.
> *Dimension:* Greatest height, 9 cm.
> *Provenience:* Old Walpi, Arizona.

FIGURE 5: No. 67142
> *Description:* Jar.
> *Dimension:* Greatest height, 15.2 cm.
> *Provenience:* West of Oraibi, Arizona.

FIGURE 6: No. 67146
> *Description:* Jar.
> *Dimension:* Greatest height, 10.5 cm.
> *Provenience:* Near Oraibi, Arizona.

FIGURE 7: No. 80949
> *Description:* Jar.
> *Dimension:* Greatest height, 11.3 cm.
> *Provenience:* Old Walpi, Arizona.

FIGURE 8: No. 80845
> *Description:* Jar.
> *Dimension:* Greatest height, 11.1 cm.
> *Provenience:* Old Walpi, Arizona.

FIGURE 9: No. 80762
> *Description:* Jar.
> *Dimension:* Greatest height, 10.9 cm.
> *Provenience:* Old Walpi, Arizona.

1

2

3

4

5

6

7

3

9

PLATE 51: SIKYATKI POLYCHROME

Kayenta Branch

FIGURE 1: No. 75395

Description: Bowl; very detailed human hand as design.
Dimension: Greatest diameter, 24 cm.
Provenience: Sikyatki, Arizona.

FIGURE 2: No. 80958

Description: Bowl; unusual beauty of design.   Shape may be unique for this type.
Both surfaces extremely smooth.
Dimension: Greatest diameter, 18.4 cm.
Provenience: Old Walpi, Arizona.

FIGURE 3: No. 111208

Description: Bowl; painting of animal inside.
Dimension: Greatest diameter, 23 cm.
Provenience: Hopi country, Arizona.

FIGURE 4: No. 72569

Description: Parrot effigy.
Dimension: Greatest length, 17.9 cm.
Provenience: Homolovi (No. 1), Arizona.

FIGURE 5: No. 67227

Description: Bowl; painting of human(?) figure on inside.
Dimension: Greatest diameter, 22.6 cm.
Provenience: Mishongnovi, Arizona.

FIGURE 6: No. 80085

Description: Bowl; loop handle; two red animal effigies perched on rim.
Dimension: Greatest height, excluding effigies, 7.9 cm.
Provenience: Awatovi, Arizona.

FIGURE 7: No. 75866

Description: Bowl; interior painting of bird(?).
Dimension: Greatest diameter, 27 cm.
Provenience: Mishongnovi, Arizona.

FIGURE 8: No. 67190

Description: Bird-effigy vessel; unusually rough finish.
Dimension: Greatest length, 17.4 cm.
Provenience: Valley northeast of Oraibi, Arizona.

FIGURE 9: No. 67123.

Description: Bowl; three human(?) figures on interior.   May date after the Spanish
Conquest.
Dimension: Greatest diameter, 27.9 cm.
Provenience: Oraibi, Arizona.

PLATE 52: SIKYATKI POLYCHROME
Kayenta Branch

FIGURE 1: No. 75422
> *Description:* Bowl.
> *Dimension:* Greatest diameter, 26.3 cm.
> *Provenience:* Sikyatki, Arizona.

FIGURE 2: No. 75508
> *Description:* Bowl.
> *Dimension:* Greatest diameter, 26 cm.
> *Provenience:* Mishongnovi, Arizona.

FIGURE 3: No. 75411
> *Description:* Bowl.
> *Dimension:* Greatest diameter, 25.5 cm.
> *Provenience:* Sikyatki, Arizona.

FIGURE 4: No. 75416
> *Description:* Bowl.
> *Dimension:* Greatest diameter, 25.6 cm.
> *Provenience:* Sikyatki, Arizona.

FIGURE 5: No. 75400
> *Description:* Bowl.
> *Dimension:* Greatest diameter, 23.5 cm.
> *Provenience:* Sikyatki, Arizona.

FIGURE 6: No. 21156
> *Description:* Bowl.
> *Dimension:* Greatest diameter, 24.1 cm.
> *Provenience:* Hopi country, Arizona.

This plate shows the size and variety of design typical of Sikyatki Polychrome bowls.

1

2

3

4

5

6

PLATE 53: SIKYATKI POLYCHROME

Kayenta Branch

FIGURE 1: No. 80749

Description: Mug. This shape is uncommon in this type.
Dimension: Greatest height, excluding handle, 9.1 cm.
Provenience: Old Walpi, Arizona.

FIGURE 2: No. 75769

Description: Oval vessel; medicine box(?). Eight carrying-cord holes.
Dimension: Greatest length, 18.3 cm.
Provenience: Mishongnovi, Arizona.

FIGURE 3: No. 80948

Description: Jar; originally had loop handle or double spout.
Dimension: Greatest height, 10 cm.
Provenience: Old Walpi, Arizona.

FIGURE 4: No. 80903

Description: Ladle.
Dimension: Greatest diameter of bowl, 14.6 cm.
Provenience: Old Walpi, Arizona.

FIGURE 5: No. 81036

Description: Ladle; half-gourd type.
Dimension: Greatest length, 19.3 cm.
Provenience: Old Walpi, Arizona.

FIGURE 6: No. 67171

Description: Ladle.
Dimension: Greatest diameter of bowl, 7.6 cm.
Provenience: Near Oraibi, Arizona.

FIGURE 7: No. 81059

Description: Ladle; concave handle.
Dimension: Greatest length, 19.7 cm.
Provenience: Old Walpi, Arizona.

FIGURE 8: No. 75562

Description: Ladle; originally had short hook handle.
Dimension: Greatest diameter of bowl, 12.5 cm.
Provenience: Mishongnovi, Arizona.

FIGURE 9: No. 80756

Description: Pitcher; unusual shape.
Dimension: Greatest height, 14.2 cm.
Provenience: Old Walpi, Arizona.

FIGURE 10: No. 80773

Description: Bird-effigy vessel.
Dimension: Greatest height, 14.3 cm.
Provenience: Old Walpi, Arizona.

FIGURE 11: No. 75415

Description: Canteen; two loop handles.
Dimension: Greatest height, 13.2 cm.
Provenience: Sikyatki, Arizona.

There are only fourteen ladles in the collection of Sikyatki Polychrome; not one of them is well executed. This may be true of all Sikyatki Polychrome ladles?

116

1   2   3

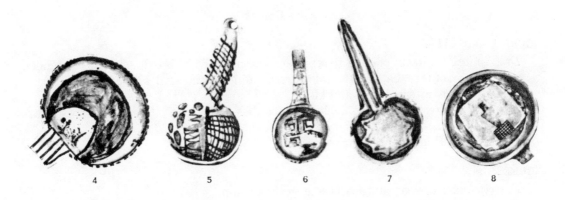

4   5   6   7   8

9   10   11

PLATE 54: SIKYATKI POLYCHROME

Kayenta Branch

FIGURE 1: No. 21174

Description: Canteen; painted to represent katcina. There is only one other specimen of this shape in the collections, and it is decorated with concentric circles of alternate red and black.

Dimension: Greatest width, including handles, 32.3 cm. Greatest front-to-rear thickness, including nose, 19.4 cm.

Provenience: Hopi country, Arizona.

FIGURE 2: No. 75429

Description: Huge jar; unusually fine workmanship.

Dimension: Greatest diameter, 34.6 cm.

Provenience: Eastern cemetery of Sikyatki, Arizona.

1

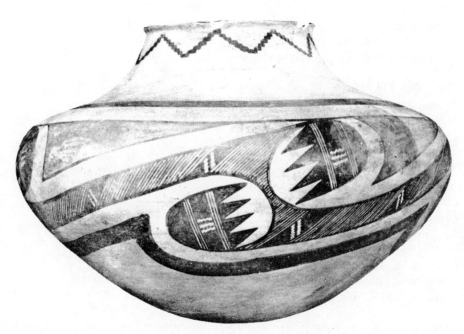

2

PLATE 55: POST-CONQUEST* SIKYATKI POLYCHROME

Kayenta Branch

FIGURE 1: No. 80839

    Description: Jar.
    Dimension: Greatest height, 11.8 cm.
    Provenience: Old Walpi, Arizona.

FIGURE 2: No. 80216

    Description: Jar.
    Dimension: Greatest height, 7.9 cm.
    Provenience: Awatovi, Arizona.

FIGURE 3: No. 80857

    Description: Jar.
    Dimension: Greatest height, 10.8 cm.
    Provenience: Old Walpi, Arizona.

FIGURE 4: No. 80641

    Description: Jar.
    Dimension: Greatest height, 11.1 cm.
    Provenience: Old Walpi, Arizona.

FIGURE 5: No. 67208

    Description: Jar.
    Dimension: Greatest height, 11 cm.
    Provenience: Near Oraibi, Arizona.

FIGURE 6: No. 81215

    Description: Jar.
    Dimension: Greatest height, 8.7 cm.
    Provenience: Old Walpi, Arizona.

FIGURE 7: No. 21170

    Description: Jar.
    Dimension: Greatest height, 10 cm.
    Provenience: Hopi country, Arizona.

FIGURE 8: No. 80951

    Description: Jar.
    Dimension: Greatest height, 9.2 cm.
    Provenience: Old Walpi, Arizona.

FIGURE 9: No. 80693

    Description: Jar.
    Dimension: Greatest height, 9.7 cm.
    Provenience: Old Walpi, Arizona.

*May be earlier, as poorly executed specimens are known from Pre-Conquest times.

1

2

3

4

5

6

7

8

9

PLATE 56: POST-CONQUEST(?) HOPI POTTERY

Kayenta Branch

FIGURE 1: No. 80825
> *Description:* Pitcher; two handles.
> *Dimension:* Greatest height, 9.1 cm.
> *Provenience:* Old Walpi, Arizona.

FIGURE 2: No. 50739
> *Description:* Bowl; showing both Zuñi and Hopi traits.
> *Dimension:* Greatest diameter, 29.2 cm.
> *Provenience:* Cliff house, near McElmo Canyon, Utah.

FIGURE 3: No. 81549
> *Description:* Incurved bowl; finish not smooth.
> *Dimension:* Greatest height, 8 cm.
> *Provenience:* Unknown.

FIGURE 4: No. 80957
> *Description:* Bowl; very shallow; finish not smooth.
> *Dimension:* Greatest diameter, 13.7 cm.
> *Provenience:* Old Walpi, Arizona.

FIGURE 5: No. 67141
> *Description:* Large jar.
> *Dimension:* Greatest diameter, 35.8 cm.
> *Provenience:* Just west of Oraibi, Arizona.

FIGURE 6: No. 21127
> *Description:* Bowl.
> *Dimension:* Greatest diameter, 13.2 cm.
> *Provenience:* Hopi country, Arizona.

FIGURE 7: No. 67147
> *Description:* Eccentric-shaped rectangular jar.
> *Dimension:* Greatest length, 8.7 cm.
> *Provenience:* Near Oraibi, Arizona.

FIGURE 8: No. 81468
> *Description:* Bowl; finish not smooth.
> *Dimension:* Greatest diameter, 20.4 cm.
> *Provenience:* Payupki, Arizona.

FIGURE 9: No. 67168
> *Description:* Bowl; finish not smooth.
> *Dimension:* Greatest diameter, 16.5 cm.
> *Provenience:* East edge of Oraibi, Arizona.

FIGURE 10: No. 67154
> *Description:* Rectangular bowl; strap handle on long side.
> *Dimension:* Greatest length, 9.7 cm.
> *Provenience:* Hopi country

II. MESA VERDE BRANCH

Pottery of the Mesa Verde Branch is found in the "Four Corners District" (that region around the common meeting point of Utah, Colorado, Arizona, and New Mexico). The branch receives its name from Mesa Verde National Park in Colorado where most of the Mesa Verde types were first found. The later pottery of this branch traveled down into Chaco Canyon, to Bernalillo, New Mexico, and into Canyons del Muerto and de Chelly, Arizona.

The type of paint on the Black-on-White pottery of this branch varied from time to time. The earliest painted pottery, called Basket Maker or Lino Black-on-Gray, was decorated with either mineral or organic paints. Mancos Black-on-White shows only mineral paint; McElmo Black-on-White, either mineral or organic paint. The paint on Abajo Red-on-Orange is hematite; and on La Plata Black-on-Orange (a late variant of Abajo) it is iron manganese (Morris and Shepard, pp. 270–271).

The designs on Lino Black-on-Gray (none illustrated) in this branch are very similar to Lino Black-on-Gray designs from other branches. There seems to be no connection, however, between Lino and Mancos Black-on-White designs. Mancos Black-on-White pottery, even from earliest times, manifests the same general appearance, treatment, and elements of design as early Chaco pottery (Martin, 1938, Plates 147–175). Mancos Black-on-White is probably the result of influences from the Chaco area.

The origin of the color and designs on Abajo Red-on-Orange and La Plata Black-on-Orange is a moot point. Some of the designs on these wares certainly resemble those on Lino Black-on-Gray pottery. Others bear a similarity to designs found on southern orange wares. We believe that the idea for the orange color and the polished surface treatment came from the south (Mogollon?).

The Black-on-White pottery of the Mesa Verde Branch shows three characteristics which are certainly unusual if not unique.

(1) Waxy, highly polished, crackled surfaces are typical of Mesa Verde Black-on-White.

(2) Mesa Verde Black-on-White bowls are generally thick-walled, with flat, ticked rims.

(3) "Beer-mug" shapes were invented and more fully developed than in any other branch. In fact, only in the Kayenta Branch do we find similar shapes; elsewhere they are lacking in the collection.

The number of types that can be classified as belonging to the Mesa Verde Branch is comparatively small. The pottery types illustrated are generally dated as follows:

	Estimated date A. D.		Estimated date A. D.
Lino Black-on-Gray	600–900	Mancos Black-on-White	850–1100
Abajo Red-on-Orange	700–900	McElmo Black-on-White	900–1100
La Plata Black-on-Orange	800–950	Mesa Verde Black-on-White	1150–1300

PLATE 57: ABAJO RED-ON-ORANGE AND LA PLATA BLACK-ON-ORANGE
Mesa Verde Branch

FIGURE 1: No. 74855

Description: Bowl; flat, painted rim. Abajo Red-on-Orange.
Dimension: Greatest diameter, 19.6 cm.
Provenience: Ojo Bonito, New Mexico.

FIGURE 2: No. 206001

Description: Gourd-shaped jar; La Plata Black-on-Orange.
Dimension: Greatest height, 11 cm.
Provenience: Near Cortez, Colorado. Exchange with F. F. McArthur.

FIGURE 3: No. 81536

Description: Bowl; La Plata(?) Black-on-Orange.
Dimension: Greatest diameter, 17.6 cm.
Provenience: Chaco Canyon, New Mexico.

FIGURE 4: No. 47769

Description: Gourd-shaped jar; La Plata(?) Black-on-Orange.
Dimension: Greatest height, 12.7 cm.
Provenience: Near Ackmen, Colorado.

FIGURE 5: No. 206286

Description: Basket-handled bowl; La Plata Black-on-Orange.
Dimension: Greatest height, excluding handle, 10.2 cm.
Provenience: Near Pleasant View, Colorado.

FIGURE 6: No. 47770

Description: Seed jar; two lug handles perforated vertically. Light material is restoration. Abajo Red-on-Orange.
Dimension: Greatest height, 12.9 cm.
Provenience: Near Ackmen, Colorado.

FIGURE 7: No. 206323

Description: Bowl; light material showing in front is restoration. Abajo Red-on-Orange.
Dimension: Greatest diameter (restored), 24 cm.
Provenience: Near Pleasant View, Colorado.

FIGURE 8: No. 206287

Description: Bowl; Abajo Red-on-Orange.
Dimension: Greatest diameter, 20.5 cm.
Provenience: Near Pleasant View, Colorado.

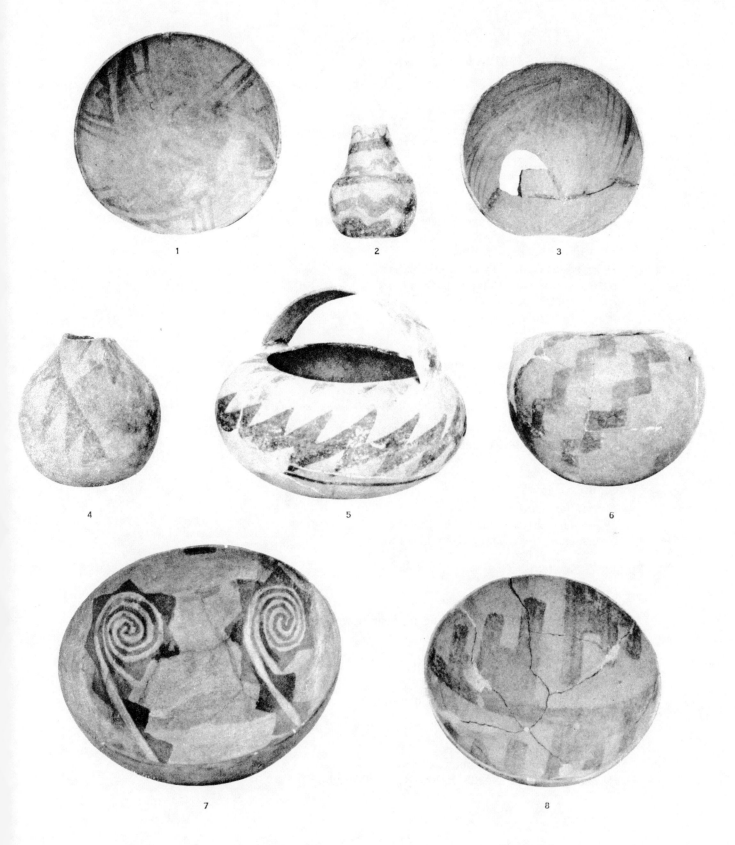

PLATE 58: MANCOS BLACK-ON-WHITE

Mesa Verde Branch

FIGURE 1: No. 81818

>*Description:* Bowl. Type uncertain.
>*Dimension:* Greatest diameter, 21.2 cm.
>*Provenience:* Chaco Canyon, New Mexico.

FIGURE 2: No. 81813

>*Description:* Bowl. Type uncertain.
>*Dimension:* Greatest diameter, 13 cm.
>*Provenience:* Chaco Canyon, New Mexico.

FIGURE 3: No. 81553

>*Description:* Bowl. Type uncertain.
>*Dimension:* Greatest diameter, 26.5 cm.
>*Provenience:* Chaco Canyon, New Mexico.

FIGURE 4: No. 45601

>*Description:* Bowl.
>*Dimension:* Greatest diameter, 19.4 cm.
>*Provenience:* Near Lowry Ruin, Colorado.

FIGURE 5: No. 205994

>*Description:* Bowl; hump-backed flute-player in center.
>*Dimension:* Greatest diameter, 18.8 cm.
>*Provenience:* Bug Canyon, Utah.

FIGURE 6: No. 45575

>*Description:* Bowl.
>*Dimension:* Greatest diameter, 19.6 cm.
>*Provenience:* Near Lowry Ruin, Colorado.

FIGURE 7: No. 45312

>*Description:* Bowl.
>*Dimension:* Greatest diameter, 16 cm.
>*Provenience:* Burial on Herren Farm, near Lowry Ruin, Colorado.

FIGURE 8: No. 45600

>*Description:* Bowl; very heavy walls.
>*Dimension:* Greatest diameter, 26.6 cm.
>*Provenience:* Near Lowry Ruin, Colorado.

FIGURE 9: No. 45410

>*Description:* Bowl; thick walls.
>*Dimension:* Greatest diameter, 20.8 cm.
>*Provenience:* Burial No. 28, Lowry Ruin, Colorado.

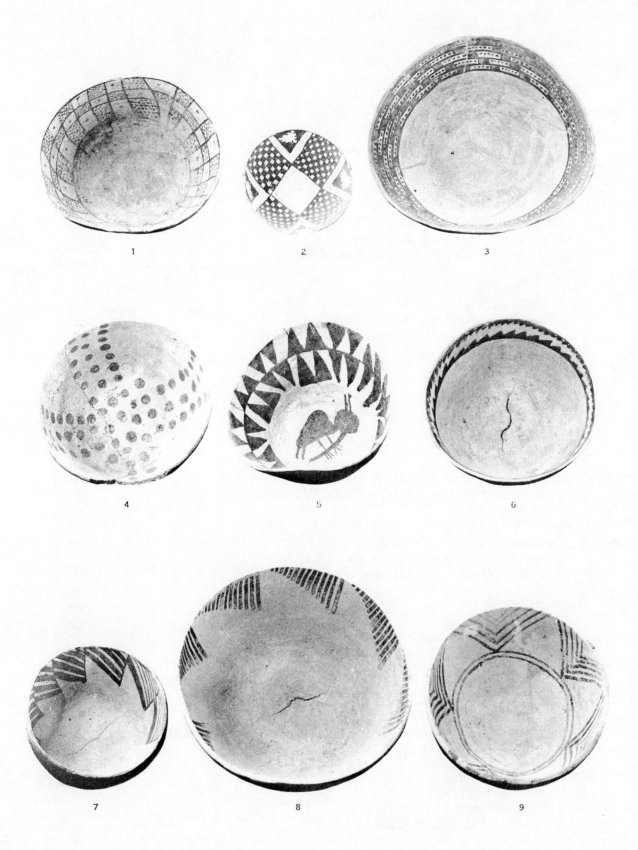

1

2

3

4

5

6

7

8

9

PLATE 59: MANCOS BLACK-ON-WHITE
Mesa Verde Branch

FIGURE 1: No. 45584

Description: Pitcher.
Dimension: Greatest height, 14.9 cm.
Provenience: Near Lowry Ruin, Colorado.

FIGURE 2: No. 205996

Description: Bowl.   Type uncertain.
Dimension: Greatest diameter, 20.1 cm.
Provenience: Bug Canyon, Utah.

FIGURE 3: No. 45400

Description: Pitcher.
Dimension: Greatest height, 16.1 cm.
Provenience: Burial No. 8, Lowry Ruin, Colorado.

FIGURE 4: No. 45301

Description: Ladle.   Type uncertain.
Dimension: Greatest length, 25.8 cm.
Provenience: Burial No. 15, Lowry Ruin, Colorado.

FIGURE 5: No. 45313

Description: Ladle.
Dimension: Greatest diameter of bowl, 10.6 cm.
Provenience: Burial No. 22, Lowry Ruin, Colorado.

FIGURE 6: No. 45299

Description: Ladle.
Dimension: Greatest diameter of bowl, 13.4 cm.
Provenience: Burial No. 12, Lowry Ruin, Colorado.

FIGURE 7: No. 45302

Description: Ladle.
Dimension: Greatest length, 30.4 cm.
Provenience: Burial No. 14, Lowry Ruin, Colorado.

FIGURE 8: No. 45317

Description: Canteen.
Dimension: Greatest height, 15.4 cm.
Provenience: Burial No. 14, Lowry Ruin, Colorado.

FIGURE 9: No. 206332

Description: Mug; handle missing.
Dimension: Greatest height, 12.2 cm.
Provenience: Refuse mound, Closson Site, five and one-half miles west of Pleasant
View, Colorado.

FIGURE 10: No. 205997

Description: Seed jar.
Dimension: Greatest height, 11.6 cm.
Provenience: Bug Canyon, Utah.

PLATE 60: McELMO BLACK-ON-WHITE

Mesa Verde Branch

FIGURE 1: No. 45403

> *Description:* Mug.
> *Dimension:* Greatest height, 10 cm.
> *Provenience:* Burial No. 13, Lowry Ruin, Colorado.

FIGURE 2: No. 206335

> *Description:* Mug.
> *Dimension:* Greatest height, 7.9 cm.
> *Provenience:* Refuse mound, Closson Site, five and one-half miles west of Pleasant View, Colorado.

FIGURE 3: No. 21742

> *Description:* Mug.
> *Dimension:* Greatest height, 9.2 cm.
> *Provenience:* McElmo Canyon, Colorado.

FIGURE 4: No. 45573

> *Description:* Mug.
> *Dimension:* Greatest height, 11.1 cm.
> *Provenience:* Burial near Lowry Ruin, Colorado.

FIGURE 5: No. 45402

> *Description:* Mug.
> *Dimension:* Greatest height, 11.2 cm.
> *Provenience:* Burial No. 17, Lowry Ruin, Colorado.

FIGURE 6: No. 45303

> *Description:* Mug.
> *Dimension:* Greatest height, 8 cm.
> *Provenience:* Burial No. 18, Lowry Ruin, Colorado.

FIGURE 7: No. 45321

> *Description:* Mug.
> *Dimension:* Greatest height, 11.7 cm.
> *Provenience:* Burial No. 21, Lowry Ruin, Colorado.

FIGURE 8: No. 205992

> *Description:* Mug.
> *Dimension:* Greatest height, 11.8 cm.
> *Provenience:* Montezuma County, Colorado.

FIGURE 9: No. 45578

> *Description:* Mug.
> *Dimension:* Greatest height, 12.6 cm.
> *Provenience:* Burial near Lowry Ruin, Colorado.

1

2

3

4

5

6

7

8

9

PLATE 61: McELMO BLACK-ON-WHITE

Mesa Verde Branch

FIGURE 1: No. 21751
> *Description:* Bowl.
> *Dimension:* Greatest diameter, 19.1 cm.
> *Provenience:* San Juan River, Utah.

FIGURE 2: No. 81574
> *Description:* Bowl.
> *Dimension:* Greatest diameter, 20.5 cm.
> *Provenience:* Chaco Canyon, New Mexico.

FIGURE 3: No. 45574
> *Description:* Bowl.
> *Dimension:* Greatest diameter, 18.1 cm.
> *Provenience:* Burial near Lowry Ruin, Colorado.

FIGURE 4: No. 21432
> *Description:* Bowl.
> *Dimension:* Greatest diameter, 18.3 cm.
> *Provenience:* Graham Canyon, San Juan County, Utah.

FIGURE 5: No. 47638
> *Description:* Bowl.
> *Dimension:* Greatest diameter, 21.9 cm.
> *Provenience:* Near Lowry Ruin, Colorado.

FIGURE 6: No. 45316
> *Description:* Bowl; much warped.
> *Dimension:* Greatest diameter, 21.2 cm.
> *Provenience:* Burial No. 26, Lowry Ruin, Colorado.

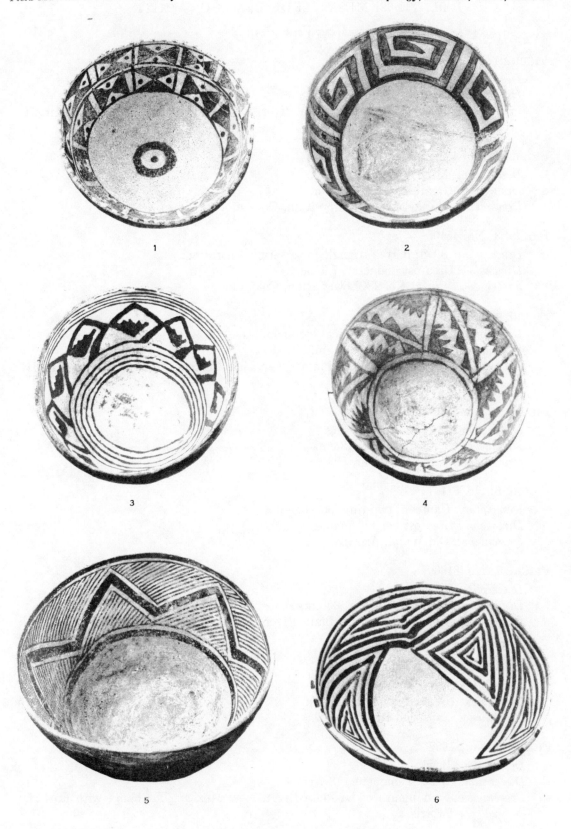

PLATE 62: MESA VERDE BLACK-ON-WHITE

Mesa Verde Branch

FIGURE 1: No. 81655

> *Description:* Bowl.
> *Dimension:* Greatest diameter, 17.5 cm.
> *Provenience:* Near mouth of La Plata River, New Mexico.   Exchange with Earl H. Morris.

FIGURE 2: No. 45292

> *Description:* Mug.
> *Dimension:* Greatest height, 8.5 cm.
> *Provenience:* Burial No. 14, Lowry Ruin, Colorado.

FIGURE 3: No. 45408

> *Description:* Bowl; barred triangle for exterior decoration.
> *Dimension:* Greatest diameter, 7.6 cm.
> *Provenience:* Burial No. 28, Lowry Ruin, Colorado.

FIGURE 4: No. 81661

> *Description:* Canteen; two vertical loop handles.
> *Dimension:* Greatest height, 9.1 cm.
> *Provenience:* Near mouth of La Plata River, New Mexico.   Exchange with Earl H. Morris.

FIGURE 5: No. 21394

> *Description:* Mug; handle missing.
> *Dimension:* Greatest height, 12 cm.
> *Provenience:* San Juan River, Utah.

FIGURE 6: No. 81141

> *Description:* Canteen; two tiny loop handles.
> *Dimension:* Greatest height, 7 cm.
> *Provenience:* Old Walpi, Arizona.

FIGURE 7: No. 81660

> *Description:* Bowl.
> *Dimension:* Greatest diameter, 20 cm.
> *Provenience:* Near mouth of La Plata River, New Mexico.   Exchange with Earl H. Morris.

FIGURE 8: No. 21756

> *Description:* Bowl.
> *Dimension:* Greatest diameter, 13 cm.
> *Provenience:* San Juan River, Utah.

FIGURE 9: No. 81657

> *Description:* Bowl.
> *Dimension:* Greatest diameter, 18.7 cm.
> *Provenience:* Near mouth of La Plata River, New Mexico.   Exchange with Earl H. Morris.

PLATE 63: MESA VERDE BLACK-ON-WHITE

Mesa Verde Branch

FIGURE 1: No. 21225

   Description: Bowl.
   Dimension: Greatest diameter, 23.9 cm.
   Provenience: New Mexico.

FIGURE 2: No. 45551

   Description: Bowl; bright red paint.
   Dimension: Greatest diameter, 30.8 cm.
   Provenience: Room 9, Lowry Ruin, Colorado.

FIGURE 3: No. 21435

   Description: Bowl.
   Dimension: Greatest diameter, 27.1 cm.
   Provenience: San Juan River(?), Utah.

FIGURE 4: No. 21436

   Description: Bowl.
   Dimension: Greatest diameter, 29.1 cm.
   Provenience: San Juan River(?), Utah.

FIGURE 5: No. 81662

   Description: Bowl.
   Dimension: Greatest diameter, 28.2 cm.
   Provenience: Near mouth of La Plata River, New Mexico.   Exchange with Earl H.
      Morris.

FIGURE 6: No. 21438

   Description: Bowl.
   Dimension: Greatest diameter, 28.5 cm.
   Provenience: San Juan River(?), Utah.

1

2

3

4

5

6

III. CHACO BRANCH

Pottery belonging to the Chaco Branch is found in New Mexico as far east as Taos and as far south as Socorro. It is also recorded from the "Four Corners District" (the common meeting point of Utah, Colorado, Arizona, and New Mexico); from the country around Ackmen, Durango, and Pagosa Springs, Colorado; and from as far west as Springerville and St. Johns, Arizona. The earlier types of Chaco pottery were distributed more widely than the later types, which are generally confined to a small area around Chaco Canyon, New Mexico.

This branch derives its name from Chaco Canyon, where Chaco pottery and architecture were highly developed and specialized. The origin of Chaco pottery, however, was probably not in Chaco Canyon itself but in and around the region near Gallup, New Mexico; or, and this is even more likely, within the drainage of the upper Little Colorado River.

The paint used on all Chaco Black-on-White pottery from early to late times was mineral (Hawley, 1936).

We have included with the plates of Chaco pottery some illustrations of Puerco Black-on-White pottery. The ancestry and affiliations of this Puerco pottery are not at all clear to us. It appears, merely from our typological study, that the Puerco Black-on-White and Reserve Black-on-White (Cibola Branch, Plates 75–80) were produced by two different groups of people who were receiving influences from a common source. However, this is a problem which needs to be worked on, and it can only be solved by making several careful excavations.

One plate of so-called Puerco Black-on-Red has likewise been included in this branch. We have done this because we did not know where else to place these particular specimens. The published description of this type is indefinite and confusing. The nine specimens here shown all come from the same region (near St. Johns, Arizona) and for want of a better name we have called them Puerco Black-on-Red. The two pitchers are shaped like the Puerco Black-on-White ones. Certainly this type should be re-defined on the basis of thorough excavations.

It is interesting to note that the designs on Red Mesa Black-on-White are very much like those on Kana-a and Black Mesa Black-on-White types (Kayenta Branch, Plates 2–9). From photographs it is often difficult to tell one from another. Only the color of the slip, the lack of polish, and the mineral paint distinguish the Red Mesa Black-on-White from the other two types mentioned.

The Chaco pottery types illustrated herewith are generally dated as follows:

	Estimated date A.D.		Estimated date A.D.
Kiatuthlanna Black-on-White...	? –850	Puerco Black-on-White........	850–1000
Red Mesa Black-on-White......	850–950	Puerco Black-on-Red..........	950–1150
		Chaco Black-on-White.........	950–1150

Wingate Black-on-Red, which is generally included in this branch, will be found illustrated and discussed under the Cibola Branch (p. 164).

PLATE 64: KIATUTHLANNA (?) BLACK-ON-WHITE

Chaco Branch

FIGURE 1: No. 74828

> *Description:* Canteen; two lug handles perforated vertically.
> *Dimension:* Greatest height, 13.2 cm.
> *Provenience:* Ojo Bonito, New Mexico.

FIGURE 2: No. 81795

> *Description:* Pitcher. Type uncertain.
> *Dimension:* Greatest height, 17 cm.
> *Provenience:* Chaco Canyon, New Mexico.

FIGURE 3: No. 74183

> *Description:* Bowl; very thin walls.
> *Dimension:* Greatest diameter, 21.3 cm.
> *Provenience:* San Cosmos, Arizona.

FIGURE 4: No. 74556

> *Description:* Eccentric double vessel, with hollow shaft.
> *Dimension:* Greatest length, 21 cm.
> *Provenience:* Ojo Caliente, New Mexico.

FIGURE 5: No. 75118

> *Description:* Bowl. Type uncertain.
> *Dimension:* Greatest diameter, 15.7 cm.
> *Provenience:* Mesa Redonda, Arizona.

Chaco Branch

FIGURE 1: No. 21406

Description: Canteen; curiously shaped loop handle. Other handle missing.
Dimension: Greatest height, 12.8 cm.
Provenience: Uncertain.

FIGURE 2: No. 92410

Description: Mug; same figure repeated on other side.
Dimension: Greatest height, 8.5 cm.
Provenience: Uncertain; notes say "Cochiti Pueblo, New Mexico."

FIGURE 3: No. 81545

Description: Canteen; two handles missing.
Dimension: Greatest height, 13 cm.
Provenience: Chaco Canyon, New Mexico.

FIGURE 4: No. 81568

Description: Ladle; half-gourd type.
Dimension: Greatest length, 13.7 cm.
Provenience: Chaco Canyon, New Mexico.

FIGURE 5: No. 21059

Description: Ladle; probably had loop handle. Type uncertain.
Dimension: Greatest diameter of bowl, 13.3 cm.
Provenience: Hopi country, Arizona.

FIGURE 6: No. 81579

Description: Ladle; concave handle.
Dimension: Greatest length, 12.9 cm.
Provenience: Chaco Canyon, New Mexico.

FIGURE 7: No. 81566

Description: Ladle; half-gourd type.
Dimension: Greatest length, 12.7 cm.
Provenience: Chaco Canyon, New Mexico.

FIGURE 8: No. 74571

Description: Canteen; mushroom handles. Hachured, open rectangle on flat base.
Dimension: Greatest height, 10.6 cm.
Provenience: Ojo Caliente, New Mexico.

FIGURE 9: No. 81806

Description: Mug.
Dimension: Greatest height, 8.4 cm.
Provenience: Chaco Canyon, New Mexico.

FIGURE 10: No. 74600

Description: Pitcher. Type uncertain, possibly Puerco Black-on-White.
Dimension: Greatest height, 10.7 cm.
Provenience: Ojo Caliente, New Mexico.

1

2

3

4

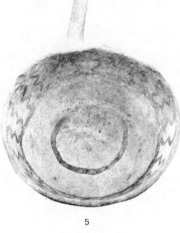

5

6

7

8

9

10

PLATE 66: RED MESA BLACK-ON-WHITE
Chaco Branch

FIGURE 1: No. 81580
Description: Pitcher; pinched-in lip.
Dimension: Greatest height, 15.7 cm.
Provenience: Chaco Canyon, New Mexico.

FIGURE 2: No. 21256
Description: Olla.
Dimension: Greatest height, 22.3 cm.
Provenience: New Mexico.

FIGURE 3: No. 81518
Description: Pitcher.
Dimension: Greatest height, 13.1 cm.
Provenience: Chaco Canyon, New Mexico.

FIGURE 4: No. 81831
Description: Pitcher.
Dimension: Greatest diameter, 20.8 cm.
Provenience: Chaco Canyon, New Mexico.

FIGURE 5: No. 81807
Description: Effigy vessel.
Dimension: Greatest height, 16.6 cm.
Provenience: Chaco Canyon, New Mexico.

FIGURE 6: No. 81599
Description: Pitcher. Type uncertain.
Dimension: Greatest height, 18.2 cm.
Provenience: Chaco Canyon, New Mexico.

FIGURE 7: No. 74605
Description: Pitcher.
Dimension: Greatest height, 14.9 cm.
Provenience: Ojo Caliente, New Mexico.

FIGURE 8: No. 81825
Description: Seed jar.
Dimension: Greatest height, 21.1 cm.
Provenience: Chaco Canyon, New Mexico.

FIGURE 9: No. 81612
Description: Pitcher.
Dimension: Greatest height, 15 cm.
Provenience: Near Gallup, New Mexico.   Exchange with Gila Pueblo.

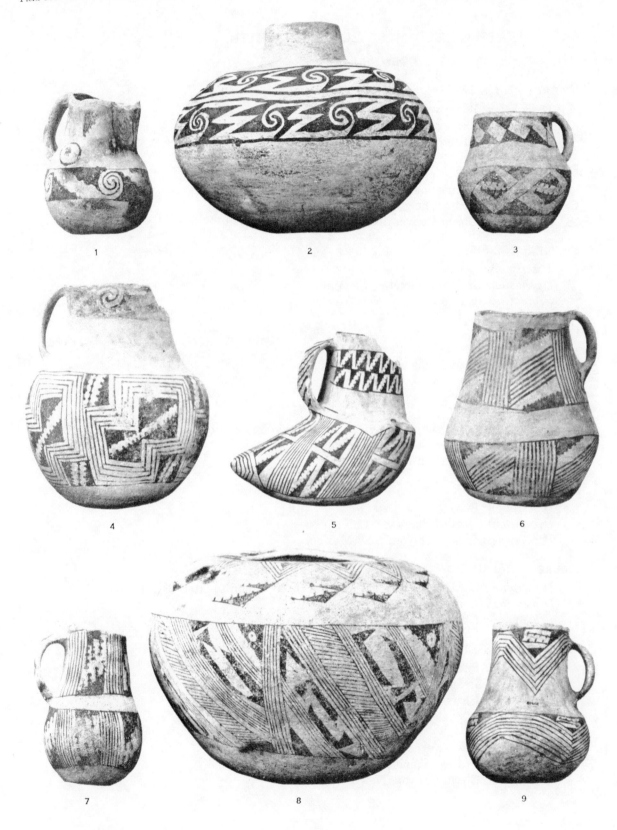

PLATE 67: RED MESA BLACK-ON-WHITE

Chaco Branch

FIGURE 1: No. 81526

Description: Bowl; warped.
Dimension: Greatest diameter, 19.4 cm.
Provenience: Chaco Canyon, New Mexico.

FIGURE 2: No. 81805

Description: Pitcher; base spherical.
Dimension: Greatest height, 15.4 cm.
Provenience: Chaco Canyon, New Mexico.

FIGURE 3: No. 81512

Description: Bowl.
Dimension: Greatest diameter, 19.2 cm.
Provenience: Chaco Canyon, New Mexico.

FIGURE 4: No. 74860

Description: Bowl. Type uncertain.
Dimension: Greatest diameter, 15.3 cm.
Provenience: Ojo Bonito, New Mexico.

FIGURE 5: No. 21065

Description: Bowl; simple ticked line decoration on exterior.
Dimension: Greatest diameter, 20.8 cm.
Provenience: Hopi country, Arizona.

FIGURE 6: No. 81587

Description: Bowl.
Dimension: Greatest diameter, 15.5 cm.
Provenience: Chaco Canyon, New Mexico.

FIGURE 7: No. 81522

Description: Bowl; artificial-looking white slip common to later Chaco types.
Dimension: Greatest diameter, 19.9 cm.
Provenience: Chaco Canyon, New Mexico.

FIGURE 8: No. 81830

Description: Pitcher.
Dimension: Greatest height, 11.2 cm.
Provenience: Chaco Canyon, New Mexico.

FIGURE 9: No. 81551

Description: Bowl; warped.
Dimension: Greatest diameter, 22 cm.
Provenience: Chaco Canyon, New Mexico.

PLATE 68: CHACO BLACK-ON-WHITE (WINGATE PHASE)

Chaco Branch

FIGURE 1: No. 81860

    Description: Pitcher; slightly concave base.
    Dimension: Greatest height, 12.7 cm.
    Provenience: Near Wingate, New Mexico (Wingate 9:1).   Gift of Gila Pueblo.

FIGURE 2: No. 81554

    Description: Bowl; warped.
    Dimension: Greatest diameter, 16.3 cm.
    Provenience: Chaco Canyon, New Mexico.

FIGURE 3: No. 81837

    Description: Pitcher.
    Dimension: Greatest height, 15.8 cm.
    Provenience: Chaco Canyon, New Mexico.

FIGURE 4: No. 81796

    Description: Effigy pitcher.
    Dimension: Greatest height, 13.7 cm.
    Provenience: Chaco Canyon, New Mexico.

FIGURE 5: No. 81834

    Description: Effigy pitcher.
    Dimension: Greatest height, 13.8 cm.
    Provenience: Chaco Canyon, New Mexico.

FIGURE 6: No. 81508

    Description: Pitcher.
    Dimension: Greatest height, 17.4 cm.
    Provenience: Pueblo Alto, Chaco Canyon, New Mexico.

FIGURE 7: No. 81803

    Description: Pitcher.
    Dimension: Greatest height, 21.6 cm.
    Provenience: Chaco Canyon, New Mexico.

FIGURE 8: No. 81502

    Description: Pitcher.
    Dimension: Greatest height, 19.2 cm.
    Provenience: Pueblo Alto, Chaco Canyon, New Mexico.

Chaco Branch

FIGURE 1: No. 81864

> *Description:* Bowl; four tiny loop handles.
> *Dimension:* Greatest diameter, excluding handles, 12.2 cm.
> *Provenience:* Tohatchi Flats (Wingate 1:1), New Mexico.   Gift of Gila Pueblo.

FIGURE 2: No. 81609

> *Description:* Bowl; large sherd missing from rim.
> *Dimension:* Greatest diameter, 22.3 cm.
> *Provenience:* Houck, Arizona.   Exchange with Gila Pueblo.

FIGURE 3: No. 81819

> *Description:* Bowl; much worn.
> *Dimension:* Greatest diameter, 13.7 cm.
> *Provenience:* Chaco Canyon, New Mexico.

FIGURE 4: No. 81507

> *Description:* Pitcher.
> *Dimension:* Greatest height, 13 cm.
> *Provenience:* Pueblo Alto, Chaco Canyon, New Mexico.

FIGURE 5: No. 81503

> *Description:* Cylindrical vase; Chaco shape and paste, Red Mesa Black-on-White
> design, and organic paint and polish of early Kayenta types.   Two
> horizontal loop handles.   Type uncertain.
> *Dimension:* Greatest height, 21 cm.
> *Provenience:* Pueblo Alto, Chaco Canyon, New Mexico.

FIGURE 6: No. 81504

> *Description:* Cylindrical vase; two lug handles perforated vertically.
> *Dimension:* Greatest height, 20.2 cm.
> *Provenience:* Pueblo Alto, Chaco Canyon, New Mexico.

FIGURE 7: No. 81506

> *Description:* Pitcher.
> *Dimension:* Greatest height, 14.1 cm.
> *Provenience:* Pueblo Alto, Chaco Canyon, New Mexico.

FIGURE 8: No. 81835

> *Description:* Pitcher.
> *Dimension:* Greatest height, 21.4 cm.
> *Provenience:* Chaco Canyon, New Mexico.

FIGURE 9: No. 205998

> *Description:* Ladle.
> *Dimension:* Greatest length, 28.2 cm.
> *Provenience:* Bug Canyon, Utah.

FIGURE 10: No. 74604

> *Description:* Pitcher.
> *Dimension:* Greatest height, 21.7 cm.
> *Provenience:* Ojo Caliente, New Mexico.

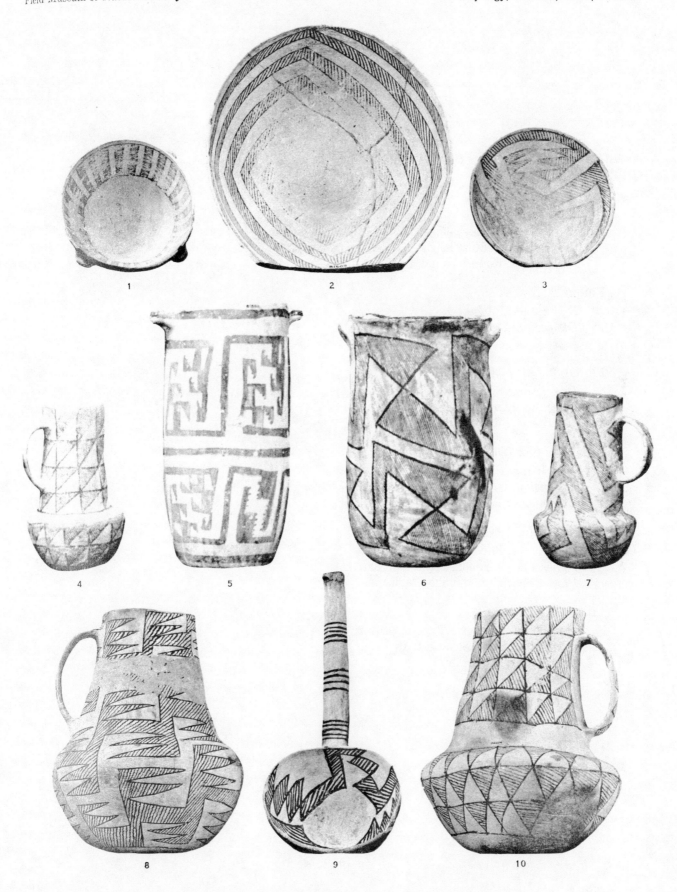

PLATE 70: PUERCO BLACK-ON-WHITE
Chaco Branch

FIGURE 1: No. 75004

Description: Pitcher; effigy handle.   Type uncertain.
Dimension: Greatest height, 17.1 cm.
Provenience: Round Valley, Arizona.

FIGURE 2: No. 73746

Description: Pitcher.
Dimension: Greatest height, 17.5 cm.
Provenience: San Cosmos, Arizona.

FIGURE 3: No. 75007

Description: Pitcher; ridge around shoulder.
Dimension: Greatest height, 15.4 cm.
Provenience: Round Valley, Arizona.

FIGURE 4: No. 75010

Description: Pitcher; effigy handle.
Dimension: Greatest height, 14.9 cm.
Provenience: Round Valley, Arizona.

FIGURE 5: No. 75003

Description: Pitcher.
Dimension: Greatest height, 14.3 cm.
Provenience: Round Valley, Arizona.

FIGURE 6: No. 167972

Description: Pitcher.   Type uncertain.
Dimension: Greatest height, 15.9 cm.
Provenience: Uncertain.

PLATE 71: PUERCO BLACK-ON-WHITE
Chaco Branch

FIGURE 1: No. 74046
>*Description:* Bowl; warped.
>*Dimension:* Greatest diameter, 15.9 cm.
>*Provenience:* San Cosmos, Arizona.

FIGURE 2: No. 74078
>*Description:* Bowl; much worn.
>*Dimension:* Greatest diameter, 10.4 cm.
>*Provenience:* San Cosmos, Arizona.

FIGURE 3: No. 75115
>*Description:* Bowl.
>*Dimension:* Greatest diameter, 16.2 cm.
>*Provenience:* Hard Scrabble, Arizona.

FIGURE 4: No. 75176
>*Description:* Bowl.
>*Dimension:* Greatest diameter, 19.1 cm.
>*Provenience:* Round Valley, Arizona.

FIGURE 5: No. 75120
>*Description:* Bowl.
>*Dimension:* Greatest diameter, 11.7 cm.
>*Provenience:* Mesa Redonda, Arizona.

FIGURE 6: No. 75117
>*Description:* Bowl; warped.
>*Dimension:* Greatest diameter, 18.3 cm.
>*Provenience:* Mesa Redonda, Arizona.

FIGURE 7: No. 74147
>*Description:* Bowl; warped.
>*Dimension:* Greatest diameter, 21.1 cm.
>*Provenience:* San Cosmos, Arizona.

FIGURE 8: No. 74437
>*Description:* Bowl.
>*Dimension:* Greatest diameter, 21 cm.
>*Provenience:* Ojo Caliente, New Mexico.

1

2

3

4

5

6

7

8

PLATE 72: PUERCO BLACK-ON-WHITE
Chaco Branch

FIGURE 1: No. 73886

> *Description:* Ladle; perforated on sides and at end. Type uncertain.
> *Dimension:* Greatest length, 22.2 cm.
> *Provenience:* San Cosmos, Arizona.

FIGURE 2: No. 73860

> *Description:* Ladle; rattle in handle.
> *Dimension:* Greatest length, 31.6 cm.
> *Provenience:* San Cosmos, Arizona.

FIGURE 3: No. 73846

> *Description:* Ladle; handle has concave upper surface.
> *Dimension:* Greatest length, 20 cm.
> *Provenience:* San Cosmos, Arizona.

FIGURE 4: No. 75078

> *Description:* Ladle; half-gourd type.
> *Dimension:* Greatest length, 8 cm.
> *Provenience:* Round Valley, Arizona.

FIGURE 5: No. 73893

> *Description:* Ladle; half-gourd type. Crude decoration on exterior.
> *Dimension:* Greatest length, 12.1 cm.
> *Provenience:* San Cosmos, Arizona.

FIGURE 6: No. 74003

> *Description:* Miniature effigy-vessel; handle missing. Type uncertain.
> *Dimension:* Greatest length, 7.7 cm.
> *Provenience:* San Cosmos, Arizona.

FIGURE 7: No. 111441

> *Description:* Double jar.
> *Dimension:* Greatest height, 10.9 cm.
> *Provenience:* Uncertain.

FIGURE 8: No. 21264

> *Description:* Miniature effigy-vessel. Type uncertain.
> *Dimension:* Greatest length, 9 cm.
> *Provenience:* New Mexico.

AND

RESERVE BLACK-ON-WHITE—*Cibola Branch*

(For main representation of this type, see Plates 75–80)

FIGURE 1: No. 74898

Description: Jar; possibly Puerco Black-on-White. Walls thick and not well finished. Paint inorganic, but dense.
Dimension: Greatest height, 32.5 cm.
Provenience: Round Valley, Arizona.

FIGURE 2: No. 74597

Description: Effigy pitcher; possibly Puerco Black-on-White. Note the "wing" protuberances.
Dimension: Greatest height, 22.7 cm.
Provenience: Ojo Caliente, New Mexico.

FIGURE 3: No. 81833

Description: Pitcher; possibly Puerco Black-on-White.
Dimension: Greatest height, 20.8 cm.
Provenience: Chaco Canyon, New Mexico.

FIGURE 4: No. 81952

Description: Jar; Reserve Black-on-White.
Dimension: Greatest height, 28 cm.
Provenience: Lower Little Colorado River(?), Arizona.

1

2

3

4

PLATE 74: PUERCO(?) BLACK-ON-RED

Chaco Branch

FIGURE 1: No. 74038
> *Description:* Bowl.   Color, 5 K 11 (Maerz and Paul).
> *Dimension:* Greatest diameter, 21.5 cm.
> *Provenience:* San Cosmos, Arizona.

FIGURE 2: No. 74021
> *Description:* Pitcher; typical Puerco shape.   Color, 5 J 11.
> *Dimension:* Greatest height, 13.8 cm.
> *Provenience:* San Cosmos, Arizona.

FIGURE 3: No. 74921
> *Description:* Bowl.   Color, 5 E 11.
> *Dimension:* Greatest diameter, 21.7 cm.
> *Provenience:* Round Valley, Arizona.

FIGURE 4: No. 74913
> *Description:* Bowl.   Color, 5 H 11.
> *Dimension:* Greatest diameter, 23.4 cm.
> *Provenience:* Round Valley, Arizona.

FIGURE 5: No. 74035
> *Description:* Bowl.   Color, 5 F 11.
> *Dimension:* Greatest diameter, 16.6 cm.
> *Provenience:* San Cosmos, Arizona.

FIGURE 6: No. 74136
> *Description:* Bowl.   Color, 5 I 11.
> *Dimension:* Greatest diameter, 25.3 cm.
> *Provenience:* San Cosmos, Arizona.

FIGURE 7: No. 74159
> *Description:* Bowl.   Color, 6 J 11.
> *Dimension:* Greatest diameter, 25.9 cm.
> *Provenience:* San Cosmos, Arizona.

FIGURE 8: No. 74603
> *Description:* Pitcher; typical Chaco shape.   Color, 5 I 10.
> *Dimension:* Greatest height, 20.1 cm.
> *Provenience:* Ojo Caliente, New Mexico.

FIGURE 9: No. 74975
> *Description:* Bowl.   Color, 5 I 11.
> *Dimension:* Greatest diameter, 29.6 cm.
> *Provenience:* Round Valley, Arizona.

1   2   3

4   5   6

7   8   9

IV. CIBOLA BRANCH

The pottery of the Cibola Branch is confined, for the most part, to the upper drainages of the Puerco, Little Colorado, upper Gila, Tularosa, and San Francisco rivers and their tributaries. This vicinity includes Zuñi, Reserve, Ojo Caliente, New Mexico; and Fort Apache, Springerville, Showlow, and Holbrook, Arizona.

The name Cibola is derived from the "Seven Cities of Cibola." On the site of one of these fabulous "cities" was built the modern pueblo of Zuñi, near which are found the late types of this branch.

The paint on the Black-on-White wares is probably mineral.

Reserve Black-on-White has generally been considered as antecedent to Tularosa Black-on-White (Gladwin, 1934, p. 18); but Nesbitt (1938, pp. 81–82) is the only one who has produced any stratigraphic evidence on this point. Typologically, Reserve Black-on-White is certainly ancestral to Tularosa. We also agree with Nesbitt (op. cit., p. 138) when he says that Reserve and Puerco Black-on-Whites are related, but we do not yet know the extent of this relationship. Effigy handles appear in Reserve Black-on-White and of course are an important earmark of the later Tularosa ware. The undeveloped nature of Reserve Black-on-White as compared to Tularosa Black-on-White can be seen by studying the plates. Figures 1 and 4 of Plate 78 (Reserve Black-on-White) are interesting in that they seem to foreshadow a bowl shape which later became common in Mimbres Bold Face Black-on-White (not illustrated).

The "sprinkler" pitchers shown on Plate 86 are rare, if not unique. The miniature vessels shown on Plate 88 duplicate all the shapes and designs found in the standard size vessels.

The whole context and chronological location of the Reserve and Tularosa phases would be much clarified if several excavations in the heart of this area were undertaken.

In the section dealing with the Chaco Branch, we stated that the Wingate Black-on-Red would be included with the pottery of the Cibola Branch. Our reasons for making this shift are these:

Wingate Black-on-Red, named, described, and illustrated by Gladwin (1931, p. 29), is represented in this volume by several plates. Our pottery corresponds perfectly to Gladwin's description except that he restricts the color of his Wingate Black-on-Red to maroon, and the shapes, to bowls. The color range of our Wingate Black-on-Red goes far beyond maroon; therefore, to help those who are interested in the range of color, we have given a Maerz and Paul color reading with each caption. Furthermore, our collection contains many shapes: ladles, jars, pitchers with strap, effigy, and eccentric handles, canteens, and eccentric shapes, as well as bowls.

As may be seen from studying our Wingate Black-on-Red plates, the designs, shapes, and handles are direct copies of Reserve and Tularosa Black-on-White wares. Some close relationship between these types is very clear; for example, the red pottery on Plate 95 shows the similarity of these designs to those of Reserve Black-on-White. The pottery shown on Plates 88–94 clearly reflects the influence of Tularosa shapes and designs.

All in all, then, our Wingate Black-on-Red shares with Tularosa Black-on-White the same area of distribution and the same designs and shapes. Therefore we think it belongs in the Cibola Branch. For these reasons, the name Wingate Black-on-Red (which brings to mind the Gallup region) seems somewhat unfortunate. Had we been naming this type, our choice would have been Tularosa Black-on-Red, for both its geographical and its descriptive significance.

Normally, the type next in this branch after Tularosa Black-on-White is St. Johns Polychrome, which seems to be nothing more or less than Wingate Black-on-Red plus white designs on bowl exteriors.

Cibola polychromes became more varied and more exotic than those in any other branch.

Since Gladwin's (1931) publication appeared, several new types of polychromes have been named and described. We have included illustrations of several of these. It is possible that some of these types lie halfway between the Kayenta and Cibola branches.

The pottery types illustrated for this branch are dated approximately as follows:

	Estimated date A. D.		Estimated date A. D.
Reserve Black-on-White	950–1150	Pinedale Polychrome	1250–1325
Tularosa Black-on-White	1100–1200	Four Mile Polychrome	1350–1400
Wingate Black-on-Red	950–1150	Homolovi types	1300–1400
St. Johns Polychrome	1100–1200	Painted and Corrugated types	1150–1400
Houck Polychrome	1200–1250	Zuñi glazes	1200–1400
Querino Polychrome	1250–1300		

PLATE 75: RESERVE BLACK-ON-WHITE

Cibola Branch

FIGURE 1: No. 21240

Description: Pitcher.
Dimension: Greatest height, 19.2 cm.
Provenience: New Mexico.

FIGURE 2: No. 21229

Description: Pitcher.
Dimension: Greatest height, 19.5 cm.
Provenience: New Mexico.

FIGURE 3: No. 75144

Description: Pitcher.
Dimension: Greatest height, 16.6 cm.
Provenience: Mesa Redonda, Arizona.

FIGURE 4: No. 82083

Description: Pitcher.
Dimension: Greatest height, 16.9 cm.
Provenience: Starkweather Ruin, New Mexico. Exchange with Logan Museum, Beloit, Wisconsin. In the Starkweather Ruin report this specimen was designated in error as Tularosa Black-on-White (Nesbitt, 1938).

FIGURE 5: No. 21251

Description: Pitcher.
Dimension: Greatest height, 17.7 cm.
Provenience: New Mexico.

FIGURE 6: No. 74981

Description: Pitcher. Type uncertain.
Dimension: Greatest height, 17.3 cm.
Provenience: Round Valley, Arizona.

PLATE 76: RESERVE BLACK-ON-WHITE

Cibola Branch

FIGURE 1: No. 74592

Description: Pitcher.
Dimension: Greatest height, 15.8 cm.
Provenience: Ojo Caliente, New Mexico.

FIGURE 2: No. 21230

Description: Pitcher. Type uncertain.
Dimension: Greatest height, 15.9 cm.
Provenience: New Mexico.

FIGURE 3: No. 75013

Description: Pitcher.
Dimension: Greatest height, 14.2 cm.
Provenience: Round Valley, Arizona.

FIGURE 4: No. 75042

Description: Pitcher; effigy superimposed on handle.
Dimension: Greatest height, 13.7 cm.
Provenience: Round Valley, Arizona.

FIGURE 5: No. 75016

Description: Pitcher.
Dimension: Greatest height, 18.7 cm.
Provenience: Round Valley, Arizona.

FIGURE 6: No. 75055

Description: Pitcher.
Dimension: Greatest height, 18.6 cm.
Provenience: Round Valley, Arizona.

1

2

3

4

5

6

PLATE 77: RESERVE BLACK-ON-WHITE

Cibola Branch

FIGURE 1: No. 74834

> *Description:* Pitcher; all-over design.
> *Dimension:* Greatest height, 16.9 cm.
> *Provenience:* Ojo Bonito, New Mexico.

FIGURE 2: No. 75022

> *Description:* Pitcher. Type uncertain.
> *Dimension:* Greatest height, 14.8 cm.
> *Provenience:* Round Valley, Arizona.

FIGURE 3: No. 81851

> *Description:* Pitcher; all-over design and effigy handle.
> *Dimension:* Greatest height, 12 cm.
> *Provenience:* Near St. Johns, Arizona (St. Johns 10:1). Gift of Gila Pueblo.

FIGURE 4: No. 75008

> *Description:* Pitcher.
> *Dimension:* Greatest height, 15 cm.
> *Provenience:* Round Valley, Arizona.

FIGURE 5: No. 75018

> *Description:* Pitcher; full effigy handle.
> *Dimension:* Greatest height, 13.4 cm.
> *Provenience:* Round Valley, Arizona.

FIGURE 6: No. 74989

> *Description:* Pitcher.
> *Dimension:* Greatest height, 22.8 cm.
> *Provenience:* Round Valley, Arizona.

FIGURE 7: No. 81686

> *Description:* Pitcher. Type uncertain.
> *Dimension:* Greatest height, 20.5 cm.
> *Provenience:* Twenty miles west of St. Johns, Arizona. Exchange with Gila Pueblo.

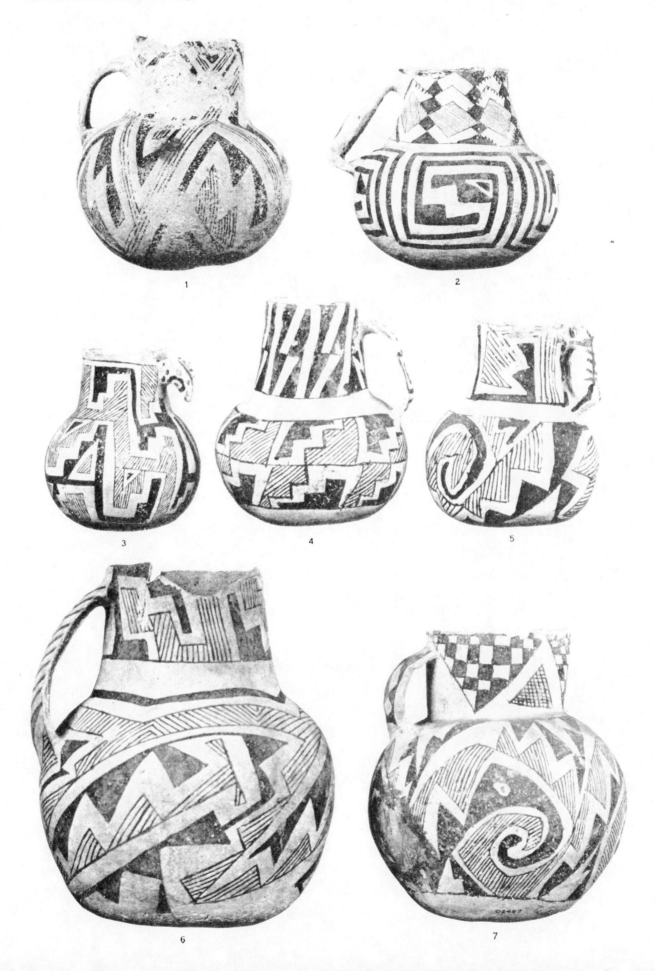

1

2

3

4

5

6

7

PLATE 78: RESERVE BLACK-ON-WHITE

Cibola Branch

FIGURE 1: No. 75177

   Description: Bowl. Note Mimbres Bold Face shape.
   Dimension: Greatest diameter, 20 cm.
   Provenience: Round Valley, Arizona.

FIGURE 2: No. 75050

   Description: Bowl.
   Dimension: Greatest diameter, 18.2 cm.
   Provenience: Round Valley, Arizona.

FIGURE 3: No. 74438

   Description: Bowl; warped.
   Dimension: Greatest diameter, 22.5 cm.
   Provenience: Ojo Caliente, New Mexico.

FIGURE 4: No. 75187

   Description: Bowl. Note Mimbres Bold Face shape.
   Dimension: Greatest diameter, 24.8 cm.
   Provenience: Hard Scrabble, Arizona.

FIGURE 5: No. 75185

   Description: Bowl.
   Dimension: Greatest diameter, 26.7 cm.
   Provenience: Hard Scrabble, Arizona.

FIGURE 6: No. 81629

   Description: Bowl; warped.
   Dimension: Greatest diameter, 26 cm.
   Provenience: Holbrook, Arizona. Exchange with Gila Pueblo.

PLATE 79: RESERVE BLACK-ON-WHITE

Cibola Branch

FIGURE 1: No. 73684

> *Description:* Pitcher. Type uncertain.
> *Dimension:* Greatest height, 18.7 cm.
> *Provenience:* San Cosmos, Arizona.

FIGURE 2: No. 21233

> *Description:* Pitcher; handle missing. Type uncertain.
> *Dimension:* Greatest height, 15.5 cm.
> *Provenience:* New Mexico.

FIGURE 3: No. 21110

> *Description:* Canteen; two vertical loop handles. Type uncertain.
> *Dimension:* Greatest height, 14.5 cm.
> *Provenience:* Hopi country, Arizona.

FIGURE 4: No. 74782

> *Description:* Canteen; two vertical loop handles. Type uncertain.
> *Dimension:* Greatest height, 16.2 cm.
> *Provenience:* X Ranch, Arizona.

FIGURE 5: No. 74567

> *Description:* Canteen; two lug handles perforated vertically. Type uncertain.
> *Dimension:* Greatest height, 13.7 cm.
> *Provenience:* Ojo Caliente, New Mexico.

FIGURE 6: No. 73936

> *Description:* Pitcher; effigy handle. Type uncertain (cf. Plate 121, Fig. 2, Snowflake
>   Black-on-White).
> *Dimension:* Greatest height, 19.6 cm.
> *Provenience:* San Cosmos, Arizona.

FIGURE 7: No. 75023

> *Description:* Pitcher. Type uncertain (cf. Plate 121, Fig. 2, Snowflake Black-on-
>   White).
> *Dimension:* Greatest height, 18.8 cm.
> *Provenience:* Round Valley, Arizona.

1

2

3

4

5

6

7

PLATE 80: RESERVE BLACK-ON-WHITE
Cibola Branch

FIGURE 1: No. 75077

  Description: Ladle.
  Dimension: Greatest diameter of bowl, 13.2 cm.
  Provenience: Round Valley, Arizona.

FIGURE 2: No. 74996

  Description: Eccentric vessel, tri-lobed.
  Dimension: Greatest height, 10 cm.
  Provenience: Round Valley, Arizona.

FIGURE 3: No. 75073

  Description: Ladle.
  Dimension: Greatest diameter of bowl, 17.1 cm.
  Provenience: Round Valley, Arizona.

FIGURE 4: No. 74830

  Description: Miniature jar; eccentric shape.
  Dimension: Greatest height, 10.1 cm.
  Provenience: Ojo Bonito, New Mexico.

FIGURE 5: No. 75024

  Description: Miniature pitcher; originally had single lug handle.
  Dimension: Greatest height, 10.6 cm.
  Provenience: Round Valley, Arizona.

FIGURE 6: No. 73792

  Description: Miniature bottle.
  Dimension: Greatest height, 9 cm.
  Provenience: San Cosmos, Arizona.

FIGURE 7: No. 73795

  Description: Miniature pitcher; effigy handle.
  Dimension: Greatest height, 9.6 cm.
  Provenience: San Cosmos, Arizona.

FIGURE 8: No. 75033

  Description: Miniature pitcher; animistic design on handle.
  Dimension: Greatest height, 10 cm.
  Provenience: Round Valley, Arizona.

FIGURE 9: No. 74580

  Description: Miniature pitcher; effigy superimposed on handle.
  Dimension: Greatest height, excluding handle, 9.6 cm.
  Provenience: Ojo Caliente, New Mexico.

FIGURE 10: No. 75026

  Description: Miniature pitcher.
  Dimension: Greatest height, 9.3 cm.
  Provenience: Round Valley, Arizona.

1   2   3

4   5   6

7   8   9   10

PLATE 81: TULAROSA BLACK-ON-WHITE

Cibola Branch

FIGURE 1: No. 73978

Description: Pitcher.
Dimension: Greatest height, 16.2 cm.
Provenience: San Cosmos, Arizona.

FIGURE 2: No. 74118

Description: Bowl.
Dimension: Greatest diameter, 22.9 cm.
Provenience: San Cosmos, Arizona.

FIGURE 3: No. 21235

Description: Pitcher; effigy handle.
Dimension: Greatest height, 10.4 cm.
Provenience: New Mexico.

FIGURE 4: No. 72499

Description: Bowl; panel of opposed terraces on exterior.
Dimension: Greatest diameter, 23.1 cm.
Provenience: Homolovi (No. 1), Arizona.

FIGURE 5: No. 21258

Description: Bowl; reddish brown paint.
Dimension: Greatest diameter, 10.7 cm.
Provenience: New Mexico.

FIGURE 6: No. 73759

Description: Pitcher; full-effigy handle.
Dimension: Greatest height, 14.1 cm.
Provenience: San Cosmos, Arizona.

FIGURE 7: No. 73755

Description: Pitcher; full-effigy handle.
Dimension: Greatest height, excluding handle, 16.2 cm.
Provenience: San Cosmos, Arizona.

Figs. 1–2 show use of spirals, Figs. 3–5 the terraced form, and Figs. 6–7 a basket-weave effect.

PLATE 82: TULAROSA BLACK-ON-WHITE

Cibola Branch

FIGURE 1: No. 73935

    Description: Pitcher; effigy handle.
    Dimension: Greatest height, 16.4 cm.
    Provenience: San Cosmos, Arizona.

FIGURE 2: No. 75043

    Description: Pitcher. Note complexity of design.
    Dimension: Greatest height, 14 cm.
    Provenience: Round Valley, Arizona.

FIGURE 3: No. 21260

    Description: Bowl.
    Dimension: Greatest diameter, 22.6 cm.
    Provenience: New Mexico.

FIGURE 4: No. 74157

    Description: Bowl.
    Dimension: Greatest diameter, 22.3 cm.
    Provenience: San Cosmos, Arizona.

FIGURE 5: No. 73673

    Description: Bottle; eccentric shape. Note how design conforms to shape.
    Dimension: Greatest height, 16.7 cm.
    Provenience: San Cosmos, Arizona.

FIGURE 6: No. 73918

    Description: Pitcher.
    Dimension: Greatest height, 15 cm.
    Provenience: San Cosmos, Arizona.

Figs. 1–2 have longitudinal hachure, Figs. 3–4 diagonal hachure, and Figs. 5–6 squiggly hachure.

1

2

3

4

5

6

PLATE 83: TULAROSA BLACK-ON-WHITE

Cibola Branch

FIGURE 1: No. 73715

> *Description:* Pitcher; handle missing.
> *Dimension:* Greatest height, 14 cm.
> *Provenience:* San Cosmos, Arizona.

FIGURE 2: No. 74583

> *Description:* Pitcher.
> *Dimension:* Greatest height, 13.9 cm.
> *Provenience:* Ojo Caliente, New Mexico.

FIGURE 3: No. 73953

> *Description:* Pitcher; effigy handle.
> *Dimension:* Greatest height, 15.1 cm.
> *Provenience:* San Cosmos, Arizona.

FIGURE 4: No. 74560

> *Description:* Seed jar; remnant of single handle ground down by ancient owner.
> *Dimension:* Greatest height, 11.6 cm.
> *Provenience:* Ojo Caliente, New Mexico.

FIGURE 5: No. 73670

> *Description:* Pitcher; full effigy handle.
> *Dimension:* Greatest height, 11.6 cm.
> *Provenience:* San Cosmos, Arizona.

FIGURE 6: No. 73678

> *Description:* Pitcher.
> *Dimension:* Greatest height, 14.8 cm.
> *Provenience:* San Cosmos, Arizona.

FIGURE 7: No. 74977

> *Description:* Pitcher; handle missing.
> *Dimension:* Greatest height, 14.3 cm.
> *Provenience:* Round Valley, Arizona.

Figs. 1–2 show variations of checkerboard, Figs. 3–5 use of fine line work, and Figs. 6–7 variations of cross motif.

1

2

3

4

5

6

7

Cibola Branch

FIGURE 1: No. 73768

> *Description:* Jar.
> *Dimension:* Greatest height, 15.7 cm.
> *Provenience:* San Cosmos, Arizona.

FIGURE 2: No. 74559

> *Description:* Seed jar; single mushroom handle.
> *Dimension:* Greatest height, excluding handle, 11 cm.
> *Provenience:* Ojo Caliente, New Mexico.

FIGURE 3: No. 75039

> *Description:* Eccentric-shaped bottle.
> *Dimension:* Greatest height, 10.2 cm.
> *Provenience:* Round Valley, Arizona.

FIGURE 4: No. 73776

> *Description:* Seed jar; unusual rim.
> *Dimension:* Greatest height, 11.8 cm.
> *Provenience:* San Cosmos, Arizona.

FIGURE 5: No. 73662

> *Description:* Canteen; two mushroom handles.
> *Dimension:* Greatest height, 12.2 cm.
> *Provenience:* San Cosmos, Arizona.

FIGURE 6: No. 73674

> *Description:* Pitcher; four-lobed body and effigy handle.
> *Dimension:* Greatest height, 12.2 cm.
> *Provenience:* San Cosmos, Arizona.

FIGURE 7: No. 74579

> *Description:* Pitcher; unusual shape. Single handle now missing.
> *Dimension:* Greatest height, 10.5 cm.
> *Provenience:* Ojo Caliente, New Mexico.

FIGURE 8: No. 73789

> *Description:* Seed jar. Note unusual manner in which decoration terminates.
> *Dimension:* Greatest height, 14.5 cm.
> *Provenience:* San Cosmos, Arizona.

FIGURE 9: No. 21244

> *Description:* Pitcher; four-lobed body and single mushroom handle.
> *Dimension:* Greatest height, 10.1 cm.
> *Provenience:* New Mexico.

This plate shows the major variations in shape in this type, other than the ordinary bowl and pitcher.

PLATE 85: TULAROSA BLACK-ON-WHITE
Cibola Branch

FIGURE 1: No. 73858

Description: Ladle; handle, in section, is square ∩, open side down.
Dimension: Greatest length, 23.9 cm.
Provenience: San Cosmos, Arizona.

FIGURE 2: No. 73863

Description: Ladle; perforated handle.
Dimension: Greatest length, 16.2 cm.
Provenience: San Cosmos, Arizona.

FIGURE 3: No. 73852

Description: Ladle.
Dimension: Greatest length, 20.4 cm.
Provenience: San Cosmos, Arizona.

FIGURE 4: No. 73882

Description: Ladle; handle missing.
Dimension: Greatest diameter of bowl, 9.6 cm.
Provenience: San Cosmos, Arizona.

FIGURE 5: No. 74864

Description: Ladle.
Dimension: Greatest diameter of bowl, 12.2 cm.
Provenience: Ojo Bonito, New Mexico.

FIGURE 6: No. 73883

Description: Ladle; effigy handle.
Dimension: Greatest length, 17.1 cm.
Provenience: San Cosmos, Arizona.

FIGURE 7: No. 73887

Description: Ladle; butterfly(?) in center.
Dimension: Greatest diameter of bowl, 12.1 cm.
Provenience: San Cosmos, Arizona.

FIGURE 8: No. 75082

Description: Ladle; rattle in effigy handle.
Dimension: Greatest length, 20 cm.
Provenience: Round Valley, Arizona.

FIGURE 9: No. 75085

Description: Ladle; unusual open handle.
Dimension: Greatest length, 14.2 cm.
Provenience: Round Valley, Arizona.

FIGURE 10: No. 73891

Description: Ladle; rattle in effigy handle.
Dimension: Greatest length, 19.1 cm.
Provenience: San Cosmos, Arizona.

PLATE 86: TULAROSA BLACK-ON-WHITE

Cibola Branch

FIGURE 1: No. 74839

Description: Pitcher; painted decoration inside neck. Type uncertain; may be Reserve Black-on-White.
Dimension: Greatest height, 14.5 cm.
Provenience: Ojo Bonito, New Mexico.

FIGURE 2: No. 73773

Description: Pitcher. Type uncertain; may be Reserve Black-on-White.
Dimension: Greatest height, 14.3 cm.
Provenience: San Cosmos, Arizona.

FIGURE 3: No. 75006

Description: Pitcher. Type uncertain; may be Reserve Black-on-White.
Dimension: Greatest height, 14.1 cm.
Provenience: Round Valley, Arizona.

FIGURE 4: No. 73765

Description: Pitcher.
Dimension: Greatest height, 16.7 cm.
Provenience: San Cosmos, Arizona.

The four pitchers shown on this plate possess a unique "sprinkler" type of handle. So far as our knowledge of the literature of Anasazi pottery goes, such handles have never before been reported. Each one is perforated through into the body of the pitcher, allowing water to pass easily. Figs. 1 and 2 have fan-shaped handles. The handle of Fig. 3 is a full-effigy shape, while the strap handle of Fig. 4 has an unusual double joining at its top end.

1

2

3

4

PLATE 87: TULAROSA BLACK-ON-WHITE
Cibola Branch

FIGURE 1: No. 73967

> *Description:* Ring-shaped vessel; hollow throughout.
> *Dimension:* Greatest diameter, 15.3 cm.
> *Provenience:* San Cosmos, Arizona.

FIGURE 2: No. 73897

> *Description:* Ladle; snake effigy superimposed on handle, head at bowl end.
> *Dimension:* Greatest length, 17.4 cm.
> *Provenience:* San Cosmos, Arizona.

FIGURE 3: No. 73687

> *Description:* Tri-lobed vessels, divided into three sections inside, also. All three
> lobes decorated differently.
> *Dimension:* Greatest height, 9.8 cm.
> *Provenience:* San Cosmos, Arizona.

FIGURE 4: No. 73984

> *Description:* "Sheep" effigy; four legs missing.
> *Dimension:* Greatest length, 15 cm.
> *Provenience:* San Cosmos, Arizona.

FIGURE 5: No. 73986

> *Description:* Animal effigy. Type uncertain.
> *Dimension:* Greatest height, 13.2 cm.
> *Provenience:* San Cosmos, Arizona.

FIGURE 6: No. 73988

> *Description:* Animal effigy; four legs missing.
> *Dimension:* Greatest height, 11 cm.
> *Provenience:* San Cosmos, Arizona.

FIGURE 7: No. 73985

> *Description:* "Duck" effigy.
> *Dimension:* Greatest height, 13.2 cm.
> *Provenience:* San Cosmos, Arizona.

FIGURE 8: No. 21044

> *Description:* Head of wolf-effigy vessel.
> *Dimension:* Greatest length, 9.9 cm.
> *Provenience:* Hopi country, Arizona.

FIGURE 9: No. 74555

> *Description:* Duck-shaped vessel; animal head handle.
> *Dimension:* Greatest length, 21.4 cm.
> *Provenience:* Ojo Caliente, New Mexico.

1

2

3

4

5

6

7

8

9

PLATE 88: TULAROSA BLACK-ON-WHITE
Cibola Branch

FIGURE 1: No. 73830
  Description: Miniature pitcher.
  Dimension: Greatest height, 7.8 cm.
  Provenience: San Cosmos, Arizona.

FIGURE 2: No. 73806
  Description: Miniature pitcher; full-effigy handle.
  Dimension: Greatest height, 8.5 cm.
  Provenience: San Cosmos, Arizona.

FIGURE 3: No. 73809
  Description: Miniature pitcher; effigy handle.
  Dimension: Greatest height, 7.1 cm.
  Provenience: San Cosmos, Arizona.

FIGURE 4: No. 73800
  Description: Miniature canteen; vertical loop handles, one missing.
  Dimension: Greatest height, 7.2 cm.
  Provenience: San Cosmos, Arizona.

FIGURE 5: No. 75089
  Description: Miniature ladle; snake effigy on handle.
  Dimension: Greatest length, 8.4 cm.
  Provenience: Round Valley, Arizona.

FIGURE 6: No. 73996
  Description: Miniature duck-shaped vessel.
  Dimension: Greatest length, 5.7 cm.
  Provenience: San Cosmos, Arizona.

FIGURE 7: No. 73821
  Description: Miniature jar.
  Dimension: Greatest height, 7.3 cm.
  Provenience: San Cosmos, Arizona.

FIGURE 8: No. 21242
  Description: Miniature pitcher; full bird-effigy handle.
  Dimension: Greatest height, 9.9 cm.
  Provenience: New Mexico.

FIGURE 9: No. 75034
  Description: Miniature bottle.
  Dimension: Greatest diameter, 9.7 cm.
  Provenience: Round Valley, Arizona.

FIGURE 10: No. 21252
  Description: Miniature duck-shaped pitcher; effigy handle.
  Dimension: Greatest height, 9.5 cm.
  Provenience: New Mexico.

FIGURE 11: No. 73829
  Description: Miniature pitcher.
  Dimension: Greatest height, 7.7 cm.
  Provenience: San Cosmos, Arizona.

FIGURE 12: No. 74831
  Description: Miniature pitcher; handle missing.
  Dimension: Greatest height, 7 cm.
  Provenience: Ojo Bonito, New Mexico.

FIGURE 13: No. 21247
  Description: Miniature jar; eccentric shape.
  Dimension: Greatest height, 7.2 cm.
  Provenience: New Mexico.

FIGURE 14: No. 73808
  Description: Miniature pitcher; effigy handle.
  Dimension: Greatest height, 7.7 cm.
  Provenience: San Cosmos, Arizona.

PLATE 89: WINGATE BLACK-ON-RED

Cibola Branch(?)

FIGURE 1: No. 73680

Description: Pitcher; effigy handle (cf. Plate 81, Fig. 1). Color 4 F 10.
Dimension: Greatest height, 15.2 cm.
Provenience: San Cosmos, Arizona.

FIGURE 2: No. 74017

Description: Pitcher; twisted handle (cf. Plate 81, Fig. 1). Color 4 F 11.
Dimension: Greatest height, 15.1 cm.
Provenience: San Cosmos, Arizona.

FIGURE 3: No. 74013

Description: Pitcher; full-effigy handle (cf. Plate 81, Fig. 1). Color 4 G 11.
Dimension: Greatest height, 16.6 cm.
Provenience: San Cosmos, Arizona.

FIGURE 4: No. 74009

Description: Pitcher; effigy handle (cf. Plate 81, Fig. 1). Color 4 C 11.
Dimension: Greatest height, 13.5 cm.
Provenience: San Cosmos, Arizona.

FIGURE 5: No. 74019

Description: Pitcher (cf. body design with Plate 81, Fig. 1, and handle design with
            Plate 88, Fig. 11). Color 4 F 11.
Dimension: Greatest height, 19.1 cm.
Provenience: San Cosmos, Arizona.

FIGURE 6: No. 74012

Description: Pitcher; large effigy handle (cf. body and neck design with Plate 81,
            Fig. 1). Color 5 E 11.
Dimension: Greatest height, excluding handle, 18.3 cm.
Provenience: San Cosmos, Arizona.

1

2

3

4

5

6

PLATE 90: WINGATE BLACK-ON-RED

Cibola Branch(?)

FIGURE 1: No. 74037

> *Description:* Bowl.   Color 4 A 11 (cf. Plate 84, Fig. 8).
> *Dimension:* Greatest diameter, 29.8 cm.
> *Provenience:* San Cosmos, Arizona.

FIGURE 2: No. 74049

> *Description:* Bowl.   Color 4 G 11 (cf. Plate 82, Fig. 4).
> *Dimension:* Greatest diameter, 29.7 cm.
> *Provenience:* San Cosmos, Arizona.

FIGURE 3: No. 74057

> *Description:* Bowl.   Color 4 A 11 (cf. Plate 82, Fig. 4).
> *Dimension:* Greatest diameter, 31.7 cm.
> *Provenience:* San Cosmos, Arizona.

FIGURE 4: No. 74062

> *Description:* Bowl. Color 4 E 11 (cf. hachure with Plate 84, Fig. 8).
> *Dimension:* Greatest diameter, 32.9 cm.
> *Provenience:* San Cosmos, Arizona.

FIGURE 5: No. 74192

> *Description:* Bowl; very worn.   Color 5 F 11 (cf. with one design element in Plate 81,
> Fig. 4).
> *Dimension:* Greatest diameter, 32.5 cm.
> *Provenience:* San Cosmos, Arizona.

FIGURE 6: No. 74181

> *Description:* Bowl.   Color 4 D 11 (cf. hachure with Plate 82, Fig. 1).
> *Dimension:* Greatest diameter, 32.2 cm.
> *Provenience:* San Cosmos, Arizona.

PLATE 91: WINGATE BLACK-ON-RED

Cibola Branch(?)

FIGURE 1: No. 74094

Description: Pitcher; unusual handle. Color 5 H 11.
Dimension: Greatest height, 11.3 cm.
Provenience: San Cosmos, Arizona.

FIGURE 2: No. 74812

Description: Pitcher; full-effigy handle, head missing. Slight trace of white outlines
used in neck design. Color 4 B 11. Type uncertain.
Dimension: Greatest height, 11 cm.
Provenience: Ojo Bonito, New Mexico.

FIGURE 3: No. 74901

Description: Pitcher; eccentric handle on which white paint is used. In the collection,
but not illustrated, is a Tularosa Black-on-White pitcher with such a
handle (cf. body design with Plate 84, Fig. 8). Color 5 B 12.
Dimension: Greatest height, 15.4 cm.
Provenience: Round Valley, Arizona.

FIGURE 4: No. 74016

Description: Pitcher; full-effigy handle, head missing (cf. Plate 84, Fig. 4). Color
4 D 11.
Dimension: Greatest height, 15.1 cm.
Provenience: San Cosmos, Arizona.

FIGURE 5: No. 74014

Description: Pitcher. Color 4 G 11.
Dimension: Greatest height, 15.9 cm.
Provenience: San Cosmos, Arizona.

FIGURE 6: No. 74024

Description: Jar; sub-glaze black paint. Color 5 D 11. Type uncertain.
Dimension: Greatest height, 14.4 cm.
Provenience: San Cosmos, Arizona.

1

2

3

4

5

6

PLATE 92: WINGATE BLACK-ON-RED

Cibola Branch(?)

FIGURE 1: No. 74904

Description: Bowl (cf. Plate 82, Fig. 3).　Color 4 F 11.
Dimension: Greatest diameter, 20.8 cm.
Provenience: Round Valley, Arizona.

FIGURE 2: No. 74891

Description: Bowl.　Color 4 I 11.
Dimension: Greatest diameter, 16.7 cm.
Provenience: Ojo Bonito, New Mexico.

FIGURE 3: No. 74919

Description: Bowl (cf. Plate 82, Fig. 4).　Color 4 E 11.
Dimension: Greatest diameter, 19.9 cm.
Provenience: Round Valley, Arizona.

FIGURE 4: No. 74920

Description: Bowl (cf. Plate 82, Fig. 3).　Color 4 I 10.
Dimension: Greatest diameter, 24.2 cm.
Provenience: Round Valley, Arizona.

FIGURE 5: No. 74169

Description: Bowl (cf. Plate 82, Fig. 4).　Color 4 A 12.
Dimension: Greatest diameter, 23.4 cm.
Provenience: San Cosmos, Arizona.

FIGURE 6: No. 74903

Description: Bowl.　Color 3 B 11.
Dimension: Greatest diameter, 21.7 cm.
Provenience: Round Valley, Arizona.

FIGURE 7: No. 81529

Description: Bowl; single solid design element on exterior like one barely visible in
center of interior.　Color 3 H 11.　Type uncertain.
Dimension: Greatest diameter, 15.2 cm.
Provenience: Chaco Canyon, New Mexico.

FIGURE 8: No. 74444

Description: Bowl (cf. Plate 84, Fig. 4).　Color 4 E 11.
Dimension: Greatest diameter, 22.3 cm.
Provenience: Ojo Caliente, New Mexico.

1   2   3

4   5

6   7   8

PLATE 93: WINGATE BLACK-ON-RED

Cibola Branch(?)

FIGURE 1: No. 74795

Description: Bowl. Color 5 H 11. Type uncertain.
Dimension: Greatest diameter, 29.4 cm.
Provenience: X Ranch, Arizona.

FIGURE 2: No. 74172

Description: Bowl. Color 5 E 10. Type uncertain.
Dimension: Greatest diameter, 28.9 cm.
Provenience: San Cosmos, Arizona.

FIGURE 3: No. 75136

Description: Bowl (cf. Plate 81, Fig. 1). Color 5 E 10.
Dimension: Greatest diameter, 24.9 cm.
Provenience: Mesa Redonda, Arizona.

FIGURE 4: No. 74186

Description: Bowl; sub-glaze black paint. Color 6 F 11. Type uncertain.
Dimension: Greatest diameter, 21.4 cm.
Provenience: San Cosmos, Arizona.

FIGURE 5: No. 74926

Description: Bowl (cf. design element with that illustrated in Plate 85, Fig. 8). Color
4 C 11.
Dimension: Greatest diameter, 32.1 cm.
Provenience: Round Valley, Arizona.

FIGURE 6: No. 74120

Description: Bowl; sub-glaze paint (cf. round design element at bottom of picture
with one on Plate 83, Fig. 6). Color (on exterior) 5 C 12. Type
uncertain.
Dimension: Greatest diameter, 31.4 cm.
Provenience: San Cosmos, Arizona.

1

2

3

4

5

6

PLATE 94: WINGATE BLACK-ON-RED

Cibola Branch(?)

FIGURE 1: No. 74028
    Description: Jar (for design similar in outline cf. Plate 88, Fig. 2). Color 5 G 10.
    Dimension: Greatest height, 7.6 cm.
    Provenience: San Cosmos, Arizona.

FIGURE 2: No. 73965
    Description: Ring-shaped vessel; hollow throughout (cf. shape with Plate 87, Fig. 1).
        Color 5 E 11.
    Dimension: Greatest diameter, 14.7 cm.
    Provenience: San Cosmos, Arizona.

FIGURE 3: No. 74011
    Description: Pitcher; effigy handle (cf. handle with Plate 88, Fig. 3). Color 4 G 12.
    Dimension: Greatest height, 7.1 cm.
    Provenience: San Cosmos, Arizona.

FIGURE 4: No. 73869
    Description: Ladle; turned-up end. Rattle in handle. Color 5 D 11.
    Dimension: Greatest length, 15.4 cm.
    Provenience: San Cosmos, Arizona.

FIGURE 5: No. 73861
    Description: Ladle; effigy handle (cf. handle with that on Plate 85, Figs. 6 and 8).
        Sub-glaze black paint. Color 5 H 10.
    Dimension: Greatest length, 20.2 cm.
    Provenience: San Cosmos, Arizona.

FIGURE 6: No. 73878
    Description: Ladle; rattle in handle (cf. bowl design with Plate 82, Fig. 4, and handle
        design with Plate 85, Fig. 6). Color 3 B 11.
    Dimension: Greatest length, 27.2 cm.
    Provenience: San Cosmos, Arizona.

FIGURE 7: No. 74877
    Description: Ladle (cf. with Plate 85, Fig. 6). Effigy handle? Color 4 C 11.
    Dimension: Greatest length, 16.4 cm.
    Provenience: Ojo Bonito, New Mexico.

FIGURE 8: No. 72391
    Description: Ladle; miniature, with turned-up handle (cf. fine line work in bowl with
        Plate 83, Fig. 3). Color 4 A 11.
    Dimension: Greatest length, 11 cm.
    Provenience: Homolovi (No. 1), Arizona.

FIGURE 9: No. 73675
    Description: Pitcher; four-lobed body and effigy handle (cf. with Plate 84, Fig. 6).
        Color 3 C 11.
    Dimension: Greatest height, 12.8 cm.
    Provenience: San Cosmos, Arizona.

FIGURE 10: No. 73688
    Description: Pitcher; with tri-lobed body. Color 5 G 11. Type uncertain.
    Dimension: Greatest height, 10.6 cm.
    Provenience: San Cosmos, Arizona.

FIGURE 11: No. 74015
    Description: Canteen; full-effigy handles, one missing (cf. design with Plate 83, Fig. 5
        and shape with Plate 84, Fig. 5). Color 5 B 11.
    Dimension: Greatest height, 14.4 cm.
    Provenience: San Cosmos, Arizona.

1

2

3

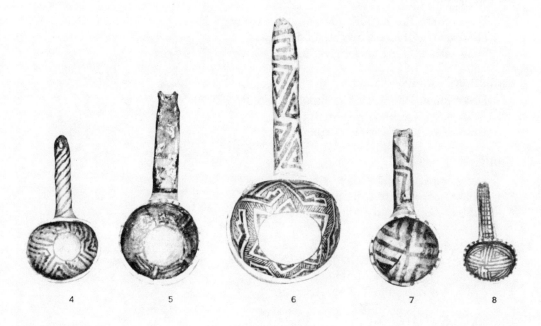

4   5   6   7   8

9

10

11

PLATE 95: WINGATE BLACK-ON-RED(?)

Cibola Branch(?)

FIGURE 1: No. 74810

> *Description:* Pitcher; handle missing. Color, 5 F 11.
> *Dimension:* Greatest height, 17.4 cm.
> *Provenience:* Ojo Bonito, New Mexico.

FIGURE 2: No. 74006

> *Description:* Pitcher; effigy handle. Color, 5 B 10.
> *Dimension:* Greatest height, 10.4 cm.
> *Provenience:* San Cosmos, Arizona.

FIGURE 3: No. 74922

> *Description:* Bowl. Color, 4 H 11.
> *Dimension:* Greatest diameter, 34 cm.
> *Provenience:* Round Valley, Arizona.

FIGURE 4: No. 74908

> *Description:* Bowl. Color, 5 G 10.
> *Dimension:* Greatest diameter, 21.9 cm.
> *Provenience:* Round Valley, Arizona.

FIGURE 5: No. 74168

> *Description:* Bowl. Color, 5 H 11.
> *Dimension:* Greatest diameter, 25.5 cm.
> *Provenience:* San Cosmos, Arizona.

The specimens here shown seem closely related, in design and technique, to Reserve Black-on-White.

1

2

3

4

5

PLATE 96: WINGATE BLACK-ON-RED

Cibola Branch(?)

FIGURE 1: No. 74897

> *Description:* Seed jar. Color, 5 F 11.
> *Dimension:* Greatest height, 18.8 cm.
> *Provenience:* Round Valley, Arizona.

FIGURE 2: No. 73790

> *Description:* Seed jar. Color, 5 F 11.
> *Dimension:* Greatest height, 12.6 cm.
> *Provenience:* San Cosmos, Arizona.

FIGURE 3: No. 74218

> *Description:* Bowl. Color, 5 F 11.
> *Dimension:* Greatest diameter, 23.6 cm.
> *Provenience:* San Cosmos, Arizona.

FIGURE 4: No. 74914

> *Description:* Bowl. Color, 4 H 11.
> *Dimension:* Greatest diameter, 28.5 cm.
> *Provenience:* Round Valley, Arizona.

FIGURE 5: No. 74796

> *Description:* Bowl. Color, 5 G 11.
> *Dimension:* Greatest diameter, 34.4 cm.
> *Provenience:* X Ranch, Arizona.

FIGURE 6: No. 74915

> *Description:* Bowl. Color, 5 E 10.
> *Dimension:* Greatest diameter, 30.1 cm.
> *Provenience:* Round Valley, Arizona.

This is the one plate included in this section which answers to the color description of Wingate Black-on-Red already published.

1

2

3

4

5

6

PLATE 97: ST. JOHNS POLYCHROME
Cibola Branch

FIGURE 1: No. 74138
> *Description:* Bowl.
> *Dimension:* Greatest diameter, 27.7 cm.
> *Provenience:* San Cosmos, Arizona.

FIGURE 2: No. 74130
> *Description:* Bowl.
> *Dimension:* Greatest diameter, 30 cm.
> *Provenience:* San Cosmos, Arizona.

FIGURE 3: No. 74164
> *Description:* Bowl.
> *Dimension:* Greatest diameter, 23.9 cm.
> *Provenience:* San Cosmos, Arizona.

FIGURE 4: No. 74132
> *Description:* Bowl.
> *Dimension:* Greatest diameter, 15.2 cm.
> *Provenience:* San Cosmos, Arizona.

FIGURE 5: No. 75194
> *Description:* Bowl.
> *Dimension:* Greatest diameter, 22.1 cm.
> *Provenience:* Mesa Redonda, Arizona.

FIGURE 6: No. 74179
> *Description:* Bowl; unusually deep.
> *Dimension:* Greatest diameter, 33.6 cm.
> *Provenience:* San Cosmos, Arizona.

FIGURE 7: No. 74114
> *Description:* Bowl.
> *Dimension:* Greatest diameter, 32.6 cm.
> *Provenience:* San Cosmos, Arizona.

1

2

3

4

5

6

7

PLATE 98: ST. JOHNS POLYCHROME
Cibola Branch

FIGURE 1: No. 74197

> *Description:* Bowl.
> *Dimension:* Greatest diameter, 15.3 cm.
> *Provenience:* San Cosmos, Arizona.

FIGURE 2: No. 74174

> *Description:* Bowl.
> *Dimension:* Greatest diameter, 19.9 cm.
> *Provenience:* San Cosmos, Arizona.

FIGURE 3: No. 74129

> *Description:* Bowl; narrow black lines used in exterior decoration.
> *Dimension:* Greatest diameter, 14 cm.
> *Provenience:* San Cosmos, Arizona.

FIGURE 4: No. 74124

> *Description:* Bowl.
> *Dimension:* Greatest diameter, 22.1 cm.
> *Provenience:* San Cosmos, Arizona.

FIGURE 5: No. 74091

> *Description:* Bowl; black paint used to outline white "paw" designs on exterior.
> *Dimension:* Greatest diameter, 22.6 cm.
> *Provenience:* San Cosmos, Arizona.

FIGURE 6: No. 74847

> *Description:* Bowl.
> *Dimension:* Greatest diameter, 18 cm.
> *Provenience:* Ojo Bonito, New Mexico.

FIGURE 7: No. 74745

> *Description:* Bowl.
> *Dimension:* Greatest diameter, 21.1 cm.
> *Provenience:* X Ranch, Arizona.

FIGURE 8: No. 74152

> *Description:* Bowl; rattle in raised center of interior.
> *Dimension:* Greatest diameter, 16.6 cm.
> *Provenience:* San Cosmos, Arizona.

PLATE 99: ST. JOHNS POLYCHROME

Cibola Branch

FIGURE 1: No. 74092
> *Description:* Bowl.
> *Dimension:* Greatest diameter, 27.2 cm.
> *Provenience:* San Cosmos, Arizona.

FIGURE 2: No. 75186
> *Description:* Bowl.
> *Dimension:* Greatest diameter, 26.2 cm.
> *Provenience:* Hard Scrabble, Arizona.

FIGURE 3: No. 74052
> *Description:* Bowl; sub-glaze paint.
> *Dimension:* Greatest diameter, 29.4 cm.
> *Provenience:* San Cosmos, Arizona.

FIGURE 4: No. 74193
> *Description:* Bowl; sub-glaze paint.
> *Dimension:* Greatest diameter, 27.4 cm.
> *Provenience:* San Cosmos, Arizona.

FIGURE 5: No. 74215
> *Description:* Bowl; sub-glaze paint.
> *Dimension:* Greatest diameter, 30.6 cm.
> *Provenience:* San Cosmos, Arizona.

FIGURE 6: No. 75134
> *Description:* Bowl; unusually deep.
> *Dimension:* Greatest diameter, 29.4 cm.
> *Provenience:* Mesa Redonda, Arizona.

1

2

3

4

5

6

PLATE 100: ST. JOHNS POLYCHROME

WITH SUB-GLAZE PAINT

(See Figs. 3, 4, and 5 of Plate 99 for more examples of this variant)

Cibola Branch

FIGURE 1: No. 74059

Description: Bowl.
Dimension: Greatest diameter, 22.6 cm.
Provenience: San Cosmos, Arizona.

FIGURE 2: No. 74033

Description: Bowl.
Dimension: Greatest diameter, 18.8 cm.
Provenience: San Cosmos, Arizona.

FIGURE 3: No. 74042

Description: Bowl.
Dimension: Greatest diameter, 23.8 cm.
Provenience: San Cosmos, Arizona.

FIGURE 4: No. 74050

Description: Bowl.
Dimension: Greatest diameter, 27.5 cm.
Provenience: San Cosmos, Arizona.

FIGURE 5: No. 74140

Description: Bowl.
Dimension: Greatest diameter, 33.6 cm.
Provenience: San Cosmos, Arizona.

FIGURE 6: No. 74080

Description: Bowl.
Dimension: Greatest diameter, 29 cm.
Provenience: San Cosmos, Arizona.

1

2

3

4

5

6

PLATE 101: ST. JOHNS POLYCHROME

WITH ATYPICAL ADDITION OF WHITE TO INTERIOR DECORATION

Cibola Branch

FIGURE 1: No. 74163

Description: Bowl; two white medallions and white base on exterior.
Dimension: Greatest diameter, 17.9 cm.
Provenience: San Cosmos, Arizona.

FIGURE 2: No. 74060

Description: Bowl; no exterior decoration.   Type uncertain.
Dimension: Greatest diameter, 24.1 cm.
Provenience: San Cosmos, Arizona.

FIGURE 3: No. 74123

Description: Bowl.
Dimension: Greatest diameter, 16.6 cm.
Provenience: San Cosmos, Arizona.

FIGURE 4: No. 74109

Description: Bowl; faint traces of white outlines on interior, no decoration on exterior.
Type uncertain.
Dimension: Greatest diameter, 27 cm.
Provenience: San Cosmos, Arizona.

FIGURE 5: No. 74087

Description: Bowl.
Dimension: Greatest diameter, 29.2 cm.
Provenience: San Cosmos, Arizona.

FIGURE 6: No. 74439

Description: Bowl.
Dimension: Greatest diameter, 21.7 cm.
Provenience: Ojo Caliente, New Mexico.

FIGURE 7: No. 74191

Description: Bowl.
Dimension: Greatest diameter, 28.1 cm.
Provenience: San Cosmos, Arizona.

FIGURE 8: No. 72205

Description: Bowl; sub-glaze black paint.
Dimension: Greatest diameter, 22.2 cm.
Provenience: Homolovi (No. 1), Arizona.

PLATE 102: QUERINO AND HOUCK POLYCHROMES

Cibola Branch

FIGURE 1: No. 74103

Description: Bowl; top and side views. No exterior light-colored slip noticeable; red slip very thick. Type uncertain; may be Houck Polychrome.
Dimension: Greatest diameter, 21.5 cm.
Provenience: San Cosmos, Arizona.

FIGURE 2: No. 74917

Description: Bowl; top and side views. Both light and red slips very thick. Querino

Polychrome.
Dimension: Greatest diameter, 22.9 cm.
Provenience: Round Valley, Arizona.

FIGURE 3: No. 74177

Description: Bowl; top and side views. Querino Polychrome.
Dimension: Greatest diameter, 21.4 cm.
Provenience: San Cosmos, Arizona.

FIGURE 4: No. 74220

Description: Bowl; top and side views. Note use of black outlines on exterior. Type uncertain, but may be Querino Polychrome.
Dimension: Greatest diameter, 30 cm.
Provenience: San Cosmos, Arizona.

FIGURE 5: No. 74212

Description: Bowl; top and side views. Houck Polychrome.
Dimension: Greatest diameter, 30.2 cm.
Provenience: San Cosmos, Arizona.

PLATE 103: PINEDALE POLYCHROME

Cibola Branch

FIGURE 1: No. 72241

Description: Bowl; white outlines for black medallions on exterior.
Dimension: Greatest diameter, 25.8 cm.
Provenience: Homolovi (No. 1), Arizona.

FIGURE 2: No. 74067

Description: Bowl; no evidence of white paint, but otherwise fits description of Pinedale Polychrome. This type sometimes called Pinedale Black-on-Red (Colton and Hargrave, 1937).
Dimension: Greatest diameter, 23.8 cm.
Provenience: San Cosmos, Arizona.

FIGURE 3: No. 74173

Description: Bowl; white outlines for black medallions on exterior.
Dimension: Greatest diameter, 31 cm.
Provenience: San Cosmos, Arizona.

FIGURE 4: No. 74029

Description: Bowl; white outlines for black panel on exterior.
Dimension: Greatest diameter, 28.2 cm.
Provenience: San Cosmos, Arizona.

FIGURE 5: No. 74095

Description: Bowl; white outlines for black medallions on exterior, some white outlines on interior.
Dimension: Greatest diameter, 33.6 cm.
Provenience: San Cosmos, Arizona.

FIGURE 6: No. 74189

Description: Bowl; white outlines for black medallions on exterior.
Dimension: Greatest diameter, 32.1 cm.
Provenience: San Cosmos, Arizona.

1

2

3

4

5

6

PLATE 104: PINEDALE POLYCHROME
Cibola Branch

FIGURE 1: No. 84771

Description: Bowl; sub-glaze black paint, white outlines for exterior black panel.
Dimension: Greatest diameter, 22 cm.
Provenience: East Fork of White River, Arizona.

FIGURE 2: No. 74807

Description: Jar; sub-glaze black paint, rim painted white, then ticked with black.
Dimension: Greatest height, 7.7 cm.
Provenience: Ojo Bonito, New Mexico.

FIGURE 3: No. 72207

Description: Bowl; black sub-glaze paint on both surfaces, exterior panel of white, with black bordering stripes.
Dimension: Greatest diameter, 22.4 cm.
Provenience: Homolovi (No. 1), Arizona.

FIGURE 4: No. 72170

Description: Bowl; black sub-glaze paint on both surfaces, white outlines for black panel on exterior, and some white outlines on interior.
Dimension: Greatest diameter, 25.2 cm.
Provenience: Homolovi (No. 1), Arizona.

FIGURE 5: No. 72147

Description: Bowl; white outlines for all of interior design and exterior panel, base color a bright pink.
Dimension: Greatest diameter, 24.3 cm.
Provenience: Homolovi (No. 1), Arizona.

FIGURE 6: No. 72185

Description: Bowl; sub-glaze black paint on both surfaces, white outlines for black panel on exterior.
Dimension: Greatest diameter, 26.9 cm.
Provenience: Homolovi (No. 1), Arizona.

FIGURE 7: No. 72243

Description: Bowl; sub-glaze black paint on both surfaces, white outlines for exterior black panel, and some white outlines on interior.
Dimension: Greatest diameter, 24.8 cm.
Provenience: Homolovi (No. 1), Arizona.

Anthropology, Memoirs, Vol. 5, Plate 104

1   2   3

4   5

6   7

PLATE 105: FOUR MILE POLYCHROME *

Cibola Branch

FIGURE 1: No. 72993

    Description: Jar.
    Dimension: Greatest height, 11.4 cm.
    Provenience: Homolovi (No. 1), Arizona.

FIGURE 2: No. 72991

    Description: Jar; three faces and a short geometric panel around body.
    Dimension: Greatest height, 11.2 cm.
    Provenience: Homolovi (No. 1), Arizona.

FIGURE 3: No. 73981

    Description: Animal effigy; four legs missing.
    Dimension: Greatest height, 12.2 cm.
    Provenience: San Cosmos, Arizona.

FIGURE 4: No. 73983

    Description: Animal effigy; base color a bright pink.   Type uncertain.
    Dimension: Greatest height, 15.6 cm.
    Provenience: San Cosmos, Arizona.

FIGURE 5: No. 73982

    Description: Animal effigy.   Type uncertain; legs missing.
    Dimension: Greatest height, 9.4 cm.
    Provenience: San Cosmos, Arizona.

FIGURE 6: No. 72992

    Description: Jar.
    Dimension: Greatest height, 11.9 cm.
    Provenience: Homolovi (No. 1), Arizona.

FIGURE 7: No. 72079

    Description: Jar.
    Dimension: Greatest height, 11.9 cm.
    Provenience: Homolovi (No. 2), Arizona.

* See Plate 1, Frontispiece, for katcina bowl of Four Mile Polychrome.

1

2

3

4

5

6

7

PLATE 106: FOUR MILE POLYCHROME
Cibola Branch

FIGURE 1: No. 72310
> *Description:* Bowl; exterior panel of white keys.
> *Dimension:* Greatest diameter, 22.7 cm.
> *Provenience:* Homolovi (No. 1), Arizona.

FIGURE 2: No. 72051
> *Description:* Bowl; exterior panel of black and white geometric elements.
> *Dimension:* Greatest diameter, 22.6 cm.
> *Provenience:* Homolovi (No. 2), Arizona.

FIGURE 3: No. 72264
> *Description:* Bowl.
> *Dimension:* Greatest diameter, 23.8 cm.
> *Provenience:* Homolovi (No. 1), Arizona.

FIGURE 4: No. 72302
> *Description:* Bowl; exterior panel of white keys.
> *Dimension:* Greatest diameter, 25.2 cm.
> *Provenience:* Homolovi (No. 1), Arizona.

FIGURE 5: No. 72719
> *Description:* Bowl.
> *Dimension:* Greatest diameter, 29 cm.
> *Provenience:* Homolovi (No. 1), Arizona.

FIGURE 6: No. 72980
> *Description:* Bowl.
> *Dimension:* Greatest diameter, 26.5 cm.
> *Provenience:* Homolovi (No. 1), Arizona.

1

2

3

4

5

6

PLATE 107: FOUR MILE POLYCHROME
Cibola Branch

FIGURE 1: No. 72306

Description: Bowl.
Dimension: Greatest diameter, 18.6 cm.
Provenience: Homolovi (No. 1), Arizona.

FIGURE 2: No. 72301

Description: Bowl; very little use of white on interior.
Dimension: Greatest diameter, 20.4 cm.
Provenience: Homolovi (No. 1), Arizona.

FIGURE 3: No. 72653

Description: Bowl; unusual use of black within exterior panel. Very little white on
            interior.
Dimension: Greatest diameter, 23.6 cm.
Provenience: Homolovi (No. 1), Arizona.

FIGURE 4: No. 73422

Description: Bowl; exterior design of keys. Almost no white used on interior.
Dimension: Greatest diameter, 22.3 cm.
Provenience: Homolovi (No. 1), Arizona.

FIGURE 5: No. 72304

Description: Bowl; unusually large amount of black used within exterior panel.
Dimension: Greatest diameter, 22 cm.
Provenience: Homolovi (No. 1), Arizona.

FIGURE 6: No. 72984

Description: Bowl; exterior panel of white keys.
Dimension: Greatest diameter, 24.6 cm.
Provenience: Homolovi (No. 1), Arizona.

PLATE 108: FOUR MILE POLYCHROME(?)

Cibola Branch

FIGURE 1: No. 73481

> *Description:* Bowl; side and top views; curious shape.
> *Dimension:* Greatest height, 8.6 cm.; greatest diameter, 14.5 cm.
> *Provenience:* Homolovi (No. 1), Arizona.

FIGURE 2: No. 72307

> *Description:* Bowl; side and top views; curious shape.
> *Dimension:* Greatest height, 8.9 cm.; greatest diameter, 15.8 cm.
> *Provenience:* Homolovi (No. 1), Arizona.

FIGURE 3: No. 72308

> *Description:* Bowl; side and top views; curious shape.
> *Dimension:* Greatest height, 8.1 cm.; greatest diameter, 14.2 cm.
> *Provenience:* Homolovi (No. 1), Arizona.

FIGURE 4: No. 84770

> *Description:* Bowl; side and top views.
> *Dimension:* Greatest height, 8.1 cm.; greatest diameter, 17.8 cm.
> *Provenience:* East Fork of White River, Arizona.

FIGURE 5: No. 72148

> *Description:* Bowl; side and top views.
> *Dimension:* Greatest height, 8.3 cm.; greatest diameter, 17.2 cm.
> *Provenience:* Homolovi (No. 1), Arizona.

All five bowls which are here shown in side and top views, seem to represent an aberrant form of Four Mile Polychrome. The walls are very thick, the red slip is heavy, and the black paint is vitreous and crackled. All the design elements are those of Four Mile Polychrome, but, as can be seen, there is little or no interior decoration.

Cibola Branch

FIGURE 1: No. 73480
> *Description:* Jar.
> *Dimension:* Greatest height, 12.4 cm.
> *Provenience:* Homolovi (No. 1), Arizona.

FIGURE 2: No. 72309
> *Description:* Bowl; exterior panel design typical of Four Mile Polychrome.
> *Dimension:* Greatest diameter, 17.6 cm.
> *Provenience:* Homolovi (No. 1), Arizona.

FIGURE 3: No. 72989
> *Description:* Jar.
> *Dimension:* Greatest height, 12.9 cm.
> *Provenience:* Homolovi (No. 1), Arizona.

FIGURE 4: No. 72998
> *Description:* Jar.
> *Dimension:* Greatest height, 13.1 cm.
> *Provenience:* Homolovi (No. 1), Arizona.

FIGURE 5: No. 72986
> *Description:* Jar.
> *Dimension:* Greatest height, 14.3 cm.
> *Provenience:* Homolovi (No. 1), Arizona.

FIGURE 6: No. 72999
> *Description:* Jar.
> *Dimension:* Greatest height, 11.2 cm.
> *Provenience:* Homolovi (No. 1), Arizona.

FIGURE 7: No. 73000
> *Description:* Jar.
> *Dimension:* Greatest height, 13.5 cm.
> *Provenience:* Homolovi (No. 1), Arizona.

FIGURE 8: No. 73333
> *Description:* Jar; slightly concave base.
> *Dimension:* Greatest height, 11.4 cm.
> *Provenience:* Homolovi (No. 2), Arizona.

*A variant of Four Mile Polychrome, wherein the necks of jars and the interiors of bowls are completely covered with white paint.

1

2

3

4

5

6

7

8

PLATE 110: PSEUDO BLACK-ON-WHITE *

Cibola Branch

FIGURE 1: No. 74662

> *Description:* Jar; both red and black decoration.   Type uncertain.
> *Dimension:* Greatest height, 12.1 cm.
> *Provenience:* Bidahochi, Arizona.

FIGURE 2: No. 73764

> *Description:* Jar; six rounded figures and one line figure arranged around body of
> vessel.
> *Dimension:* Greatest height, 12.8 cm.
> *Provenience:* San Cosmos, Arizona.

FIGURE 3: No. 73121

> *Description:* Jar.
> *Dimension:* Greatest height, 10.8 cm.
> *Provenience:* Homolovi (No. 1), Arizona.

FIGURE 4: No. 72962

> *Description:* Jar; effigy-head handle reminiscent of earlier Black-on-White types.
> *Dimension:* Greatest height, 13.5 cm.
> *Provenience:* Homolovi (No. 1), Arizona.

FIGURE 5: No. 75220

> *Description:* Jar.
> *Dimension:* Greatest height, 13 cm.
> *Provenience:* Sikyatki, Arizona.

FIGURE 6: No. 72961

> *Description:* Jar.
> *Dimension:* Greatest height, 11.6 cm.
> *Provenience:* Homolovi (No. 1), Arizona.

* A variant of Four Mile Polychrome, wherein the whole specimen is completely covered with white paint.

236

1

2

3

4

5

6

PLATE 111: PAINTED AND CORRUGATED TYPES

Cibola Branch

FIGURE 1: No. 84751

> *Description:* Bowl; McDonald Corrugated. Interior smudged and polished, exterior a reddish-brown, with white paint.
> *Dimension:* Greatest diameter, 16.6 cm.
> *Provenience:* North Fork of White River, Arizona.

FIGURE 2: No. 75159

> *Description:* Bowl; McDonald Corrugated. Interior smudged and polished, exterior reddish-brown, with white paint.
> *Dimension:* Greatest diameter, 18.5 cm.
> *Provenience:* Mesa Redonda, Arizona.

FIGURE 3: No. 75158

> *Description:* Bowl; McDonald Corrugated. Interior smudged and polished, exterior a reddish-brown, with white paint.
> *Dimension:* Greatest diameter, 12.5 cm.
> *Provenience:* Mesa Redonda, Arizona.

FIGURE 4: No. 73371

> *Description:* Jar; brownish-black paint on tan body. Type unnamed.
> *Dimension:* Greatest height, 13.8 cm.
> *Provenience:* Chevellon Buttes, Arizona.

FIGURE 5: No. 84755

> *Description:* Jar; buff-colored paint on pinkish body. Type uncertain or unnamed.
> *Dimension:* Greatest height, 16.1 cm.
> *Provenience:* North Fork of White River, Arizona.

Figs. 6, 7, and 8, following, are of a hitherto unnamed type which has been mentioned as being ancestral to Cibicue Polychrome (Haury, 1934). Interiors are smudged and highly polished, exteriors are completely covered with a light red slip, designs are executed in a darker red, and white outlines are added. We suggest for this type the name "Chevellon Corrugated-Polychrome."

FIGURE 6: No. 72062

> *Description:* Bowl.
> *Dimension:* Greatest diameter, 14.4 cm.
> *Provenience:* Homolovi (No. 2), Arizona.

FIGURE 7: No. 72286

> *Description:* Bowl.
> *Dimension:* Greatest diameter, 18.6 cm.
> *Provenience:* Homolovi (No. 1), Arizona.

FIGURE 8: No. 72288

> *Description:* Bowl.
> *Dimension:* Greatest diameter, 13.6 cm.
> *Provenience:* Homolovi (No. 1), Arizona.

1

2

3

4

5

6

7

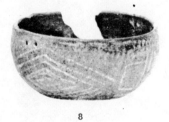

8

PLATE 112: HOMOLOVI POLYCHROME

Cibola Branch

FIGURE 1: No. 73479

> *Description:* Bowl.
> *Dimension:* Greatest diameter, 12.6 cm.
> *Provenience:* Homolovi (No. 1), Arizona.

FIGURE 2: No. 72624

> *Description:* Bowl.
> *Dimension:* Greatest diameter, 19.4 cm.
> *Provenience:* Homolovi (No. 1), Arizona.

FIGURE 3: No. 72732

> *Description:* Bowl.
> *Dimension:* Greatest diameter, 23.4 cm.
> *Provenience:* Homolovi (No. 1), Arizona.

FIGURE 4: No. 72723

> *Description:* Bowl.
> *Dimension:* Greatest diameter, 25.4 cm.
> *Provenience:* Homolovi (No. 1), Arizona.

FIGURE 5: No. 72570

> *Description:* Bowl.
> *Dimension:* Greatest diameter, 25.2 cm.
> *Provenience:* Homolovi (No. 1), Arizona.

FIGURE 6: No. 72727

> *Description:* Bowl; exterior panel of design.
> *Dimension:* Greatest diameter, 25.2 cm.
> *Provenience:* Homolovi (No. 1), Arizona.

1

2

3

4

5

6

PLATE 113: HOMOLOVI POLYCHROME
Cibola Branch

FIGURE 1: No. 72635

> *Description:* Bowl.
> *Dimension:* Greatest diameter, 23.1 cm.
> *Provenience:* Homolovi (No. 1), Arizona.

FIGURE 2: No. 72644

> *Description:* Bowl.
> *Dimension:* Greatest diameter, 24.1 cm.
> *Provenience:* Homolovi (No. 1), Arizona.

FIGURE 3: No. 52681

> *Description:* Bowl.
> *Dimension:* Greatest diameter, 20.4 cm.
> *Provenience:* Homolovi (No. 2), Arizona.

FIGURE 4: No. 72692

> *Description:* Bowl.
> *Dimension:* Greatest diameter, 18.4 cm.
> *Provenience:* Homolovi (No. 1), Arizona.

FIGURE 5: No. 72623

> *Description:* Bowl.
> *Dimension:* Greatest diameter, 23.0 cm.
> *Provenience:* Homolovi (No. 1), Arizona.

FIGURE 6: No. 72763

> *Description:* Bowl.
> *Dimension:* Greatest diameter, 23.7 cm.
> *Provenience:* Homolovi (No. 1), Arizona.

All these specimens have broken lifelines.

1

2

3

4

5

6

PLATE 114: HOMOLOVI POLYCHROME

Cibola Branch

FIGURE 1: No. 73418
> *Description:* Pitcher; small.
> *Dimension:* Greatest height, 10.1 cm.
> *Provenience:* Homolovi (No. 1), Arizona.

FIGURE 2: No. 72845
> *Description:* Mug; handle missing.
> *Dimension:* Greatest height, 10.7 cm.
> *Provenience:* Homolovi (No. 1), Arizona.

FIGURE 3: No. 73005
> *Description:* Jar; broken lifeline.
> *Dimension:* Greatest height, 11.4 cm.
> *Provenience:* Homolovi (No. 1), Arizona.

FIGURE 4: No. 73001
> *Description:* Jar; broken lifeline.
> *Dimension:* Greatest height, 11.6 cm.
> *Provenience:* Homolovi (No. 1), Arizona.

FIGURE 5: No. 73016
> *Description:* Jar; broken lifeline.
> *Dimension:* Greatest height, 17.6 cm.
> *Provenience:* Homolovi (No. 1), Arizona.

FIGURE 6: No. 73412
> *Description:* Jar; broken lifeline.
> *Dimension:* Greatest height, 14.9 cm.
> *Provenience:* Homolovi (No. 1), Arizona.

1

2

3

4

5

6

PLATE 115: HOMOLOVI POLYCHROME

Cibola Branch

FIGURE 1: No. 72266

    Description: Bowl; broken lifeline.
    Dimension: Greatest diameter, 20.3 cm.
    Provenience: Homolovi (No. 1), Arizona.

FIGURE 2: No. 73344

    Description: Bowl; broken lifeline. Exterior rim stripe.
    Dimension: Greatest diameter, 22.2 cm.
    Provenience: Chevellon, Arizona.

FIGURE 3: No. 72508

    Description: Bowl; broken lifeline and simple exterior design.
    Dimension: Greatest diameter, 23.6 cm.
    Provenience: Homolovi (No. 1), Arizona.

FIGURE 4: No. 72554

    Description: Bowl; broken lifeline and simple exterior design.
    Dimension: Greatest diameter, 23.7 cm.
    Provenience: Homolovi (No. 1), Arizona.

FIGURE 5: No. 73413

    Description: Bowl; broken lifeline and simple exterior design.
    Dimension: Greatest diameter, 22.7 cm.
    Provenience: Homolovi (No. 1), Arizona.

FIGURE 6: No. 72601

    Description: Bowl; broken lifeline.
    Dimension: Greatest diameter, 24.1 cm.
    Provenience: Homolovi (No. 1), Arizona.

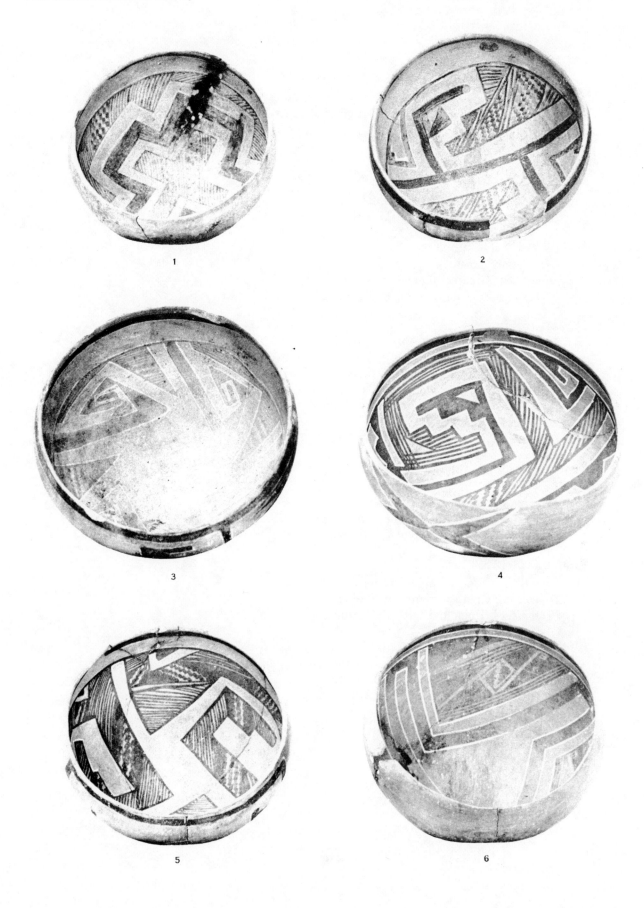

1

2

3

4

5

6

PLATE 116: HOMOLOVI POLYCHROME

Cibola Branch

FIGURE 1: No. 72751

Description: Bowl.
Dimension: Greatest diameter, 22 cm.
Provenience: Homolovi (No. 1), Arizona.

FIGURE 2: No. 72520

Description: Bowl.
Dimension: Greatest diameter, 21.8 cm.
Provenience: Homolovi (No. 1), Arizona.

FIGURE 3: No. 72803

Description: Cup; vertical loop handle.
Dimension: Greatest length, 13.6 cm.
Provenience: Homolovi (No. 1), Arizona.

FIGURE 4: No. 72693

Description: Bowl.
Dimension: Greatest diameter, 16.6 cm.
Provenience: Homolovi (No. 1), Arizona.

FIGURE 5: No. 72410

Description: Ladle; handle missing.
Dimension: Greatest diameter of bowl, 12.3 cm.
Provenience: Homolovi (No. 1), Arizona.

FIGURE 6: No. 72537

Description: Bowl; simple exterior design.
Dimension: Greatest diameter, 26.6 cm.
Provenience: Homolovi (No. 1), Arizona.

FIGURE 7: No. 72717

Description: Bowl.
Dimension: Greatest diameter, 23.9 cm.
Provenience: Homolovi (No. 1), Arizona.

1

2

3

4

5

6

7

PLATE 117: HOMOLOVI POLYCHROME

Cibola Branch

FIGURE 1: No. 72515

Description: Bowl.
Dimension: Greatest diameter, 18.5 cm.
Provenience: Homolovi (No. 1), Arizona.

FIGURE 2: No. 72572

Description: Bowl; dashes of black on exterior.   Broken lifeline.
Dimension: Greatest diameter, 17.8 cm.
Provenience: Homolovi (No. 1), Arizona.

FIGURE 3: No. 73011

Description: Jar; broken lifeline.
Dimension: Greatest height, 14.3 cm.
Provenience: Homolovi (No. 1), Arizona.

FIGURE 4: No. 72106

Description: Bird-effigy vessel; head missing.
Dimension: Greatest length, 10.7 cm.
Provenience: Homolovi (No. 2), Arizona.

FIGURE 5: No. 75640

Description: Ladle.
Dimension: Greatest length, 24.8 cm.
Provenience: Mishongnovi, Arizona.

FIGURE 6: No. 72476

Description: Bowl; broken lifeline.
Dimension: Greatest diameter, 25.1 cm.
Provenience: Homolovi (No. 1), Arizona.

FIGURE 7: No. 72048

Description: Bowl; broken lifeline.
Dimension: Greatest diameter, 23.9 cm.
Provenience: Homolovi (No. 2), Arizona.

1

2

3

4

5

6

7

PLATE 118: ZUNI GLAZES, HESHOTAUTHLA POLYCHROME*

Cibola Branch

FIGURE 1: No. 74679

> *Description:* Bowl; slight use of black in exterior design.
> *Dimension:* Greatest diameter, 20.8 cm.
> *Provenience:* Bidahochi, Arizona.

FIGURE 2: No. 74195

> *Description:* Bowl.
> *Dimension:* Greatest diameter, 24.7 cm.
> *Provenience:* San Cosmos, Arizona.

FIGURE 3: No. 74442

> *Description:* Bowl.
> *Dimension:* Greatest diameter, 27.4 cm.
> *Provenience:* Ojo Caliente, New Mexico.

FIGURE 4: No. 75114

> *Description:* Bowl.
> *Dimension:* Greatest diameter, 26.3 cm.
> *Provenience:* Hard Scrabble, Arizona.

FIGURE 5: No. 74845

> *Description:* Bowl.
> *Dimension:* Greatest diameter, 25.9 cm.
> *Provenience:* Ojo Bonito, New Mexico.

* Name applied by A. V. Kidder (Kidder and Shepard, 1936). It corresponds to Hawikuh Glaze B (Hodge, 1923). Characteristic decoration: red slip on both surfaces, black or green glaze interior design, and white line decoration (possibly in imitation of St. Johns Polychrome) on exterior.

PLATE 119: ZUNI GLAZES

ARAUCA POLYCHROME* AND HAWIKUH GLAZE-ON-WHITE†

Cibola Branch

FIGURE 1: No. 74175

> *Description:* Bowl; Arauca Polychrome. Interior design all in black glaze, exterior design of black glaze and matte red.
> *Dimension:* Greatest diameter, 22.9 cm.
> *Provenience:* San Cosmos, Arizona.

FIGURE 2: No. 74030

> *Description:* Bowl; Arauca Polychrome. Both surfaces decorated in black glaze and matte red.
> *Dimension:* Greatest diameter, 22.3 cm.
> *Provenience:* San Cosmos, Arizona.

FIGURE 3: No. 74857

> *Description:* Bowl; Hawikuh Glaze-on-White.
> *Dimension:* Greatest diameter, 17.5 cm.
> *Provenience:* Ojo Bonito, New Mexico.

FIGURE 4: No. 72968

> *Description:* Jar; Hawikuh Glaze-on-White.
> *Dimension:* Greatest height, 10.3 cm.
> *Provenience:* Homolovi (No. 1), Arizona.

FIGURE 5: No. 79376

> *Description:* Bowl; Hawikuh Glaze-on-White.
> *Dimension:* Greatest diameter, 20.2 cm.
> *Provenience:* Bidahochi, Arizona.

FIGURE 6: No. 72726

> *Description:* Bowl; Hawikuh Glaze-on-White.
> *Dimension:* Greatest diameter, 23.6 cm.
> *Provenience:* Homolovi (No. 1), Arizona.

FIGURE 7: No. 72119

> *Description:* Jar; Hawikuh Glaze-on-White.
> *Dimension:* Greatest height, 13.9 cm.
> *Provenience:* Homolovi (No. 2), Arizona.

*Name applied by Colton and Hargrave (1937). It corresponds to Hawikuh Glaze D (Hodge, 1923). Characteristic decoration: white slip on both surfaces, black and/or red on either or both surfaces.

†Name applied by Colton and Hargrave (1937). It corresponds to Hawikuh Glaze C (Hodge, 1923). Characteristic decoration: black glaze on white slip on both surfaces.

1

2

3

4

5

6

7

PLATE 120: ZUNI GLAZES
ADAMANA* AND WALLACE† POLYCHROMES
Cibola Branch

FIGURE 1: No. 74608

Description: Bowl; Adamana Polychrome.
Dimension: Greatest diameter, 23.5 cm.
Provenience: Ojo Caliente, New Mexico.

FIGURE 2: No. 74435

Description: Bowl; Adamana Polychrome.   A few touches of black glaze on exterior.
Dimension: Greatest diameter, 24.9 cm.
Provenience: Ojo Caliente, New Mexico.

FIGURE 3: No. 72026

Description: Bowl; Wallace Polychrome.
Dimension: Greatest diameter, 21 cm.
Provenience: Homolovi (No. 2), Arizona.

FIGURE 4: No. 74222

Description: Bowl; Wallace Polychrome.
Dimension: Greatest diameter, 25.6 cm.
Provenience: San Cosmos, Arizona.

FIGURE 5: No. 74677

Description: Bowl; Wallace Polychrome.   Glaze did not "take."
Dimension: Greatest diameter, 27.8 cm.
Provenience: Bidahochi, Arizona.

FIGURE 6: No. 74846

Description: Bowl; Wallace Polychrome.
Dimension: Greatest diameter, 27.2 cm.
Provenience: Ojo Bonito, New Mexico.

*Name applied by Colton and Hargrave (1937). Characteristic decoration: exterior, slipped red, carries same white line decoration as Heshotauthla Polychrome (see Plate 118); interior has white slip, decorated with black or green glaze and matte red.

†Name applied by Colton and Hargrave (1937). It corresponds to Hawikuh Glaze III (Hodge, 1924). Except that no matte red paint is used, its decoration is the same as that of Adamana Polychrome.

256

1

2

3

4

5

6

V. SALADO BRANCH

The area of greatest distribution of Salado pottery centers about Roosevelt Lake and the upper drainage of the Salt River. The name for this branch, Salado, was suggested by the name of the river. Some Salado pottery, however, has been reported from Flagstaff, St. Johns, and Holbrook (Arizona) and from localities even more remote.

The black paint on the Black-on-White ware is probably mineral.

Several years ago, by exchange, we received a few pieces of Snowflake Black-on-White pottery from Gila Pueblo. In making up our illustrations for this type, we matched up what we could from our collection with the type specimens from Gila Pueblo. There is some guesswork involved, for the reason that there is no published description of this particular ware. If our identifications are correct, it is interesting to note the astonishing similarity between this Snowflake Black-on-White and Puerco Black-on-White.

Again, we are frank to confess that we do not know just what this apparent similarity means, but we hope that excavations will help clear up the relationship of Reserve, Puerco, and Snowflake Black-on-White types. We could make some speculations, but these would be meaningless in view of the fact that so few data are available on sites yielding these types.

Roosevelt Black-on-White resembles Tularosa Black-on-White, and may possibly be an imitation of it, but again this connection is not clear.

Pinto Polychrome, as Gladwin has suggested (1930, p. 5), may have been derived from Wingate Black-on-Red.

Gila and Tonto Polychrome bear the same general color combinations as Pinto, but the designs on these two later types are very different from those on Pinto. They apparently are late specialized developments.

The pottery types in this branch which are illustrated herewith are dated approximately as follows:

	Estimated date A. D.		Estimated date A. D.
Snowflake Black-on-White	975–1100	Gila Polychrome	1300
Roosevelt Black-on-White	1200	Tonto Polychrome	1400
Pinto Polychrome	1150–1250		

259

PLATE 121: SNOWFLAKE BLACK-ON-WHITE

Salado Branch

FIGURE 1: No. 81613

Description: Bowl.
Dimension: Greatest diameter, 24.4 cm.
Provenience: Near Flagstaff, Arizona.   Exchange with Gila Pueblo.

FIGURE 2: No. 75000

Description: Pitcher; shape reminiscent of Puerco Black-on-White.   Type uncertain.
Dimension: Greatest height, 16.8 cm.
Provenience: Round Valley, Arizona.

FIGURE 3: No. 75150

Description: Pitcher.   Type uncertain.
Dimension: Greatest height, 15.3 cm.
Provenience: Mesa Redonda, Arizona.

FIGURE 4: No. 81847

Description: Bowl.
Dimension: Greatest diameter, 13.9 cm.
Provenience: Near St. Johns, Arizona (St. Johns, 7: 1).   Gift of Gila Pueblo.

FIGURE 5: No. 81611

Description: Bowl.
Dimension: Greatest diameter, 20.8 cm.
Provenience: Near Holbrook, Arizona.   Exchange with Gila Pueblo.

FIGURE 6: No. 74985

Description: Jar (cf. neck design with that typical of Roosevelt Black-on-White,
Plate 123).
Dimension: Greatest height, 14.8 cm.
Provenience: Round Valley, Arizona.

PLATE 122: SNOWFLAKE BLACK-ON-WHITE

Salado Branch

FIGURE 1: No. 73931

Description: Pitcher. Type uncertain.
Dimension: Greatest height, 19.1 cm.
Provenience: San Cosmos, Arizona.

FIGURE 2: No. 75075

Description: Ladle; handle missing. Type uncertain.
Dimension: Greatest diameter of bowl, 12 cm.
Provenience: Round Valley, Arizona.

FIGURE 3: No. 81687

Description: Bowl. Type uncertain.
Dimension: Greatest diameter, 12.7 cm.
Provenience: Tohatchi Flats, New Mexico (Wingate 1:1).   Exchange with Gila
    Pueblo.

FIGURE 4: No. 75119

Description: Bowl. Type uncertain.
Dimension: Greatest diameter, 22.5 cm.
Provenience: Mesa Redonda, Arizona.

FIGURE 5: No. 75002

Description: Pitcher. Type uncertain.
Dimension: Greatest height, 15.4 cm.
Provenience: Round Valley, Arizona.

FIGURE 6: No. 73945

Description: Ladle. Type uncertain.
Dimension: Greatest length, 21.8 cm.
Provenience: San Cosmos, Arizona.

1

2

3

4

5

6

PLATE 123: ROOSEVELT BLACK-ON-WHITE

Salado Branch

FIGURE 1: No. 75146
> *Description:* Pitcher.
> *Dimension:* Greatest height, 15.1 cm.
> *Provenience:* Mesa Redonda, Arizona.

FIGURE 2: No. 75017
> *Description:* Pitcher.
> *Dimension:* Greatest height, 15.7 cm.
> *Provenience:* Round Valley, Arizona.

FIGURE 3: No. 74150
> *Description:* Bowl; incurved, ticked rim.
> *Dimension:* Greatest diameter, 17.1 cm.
> *Provenience:* San Cosmos, Arizona.

FIGURE 4: No. 74070
> *Description:* Bowl; incurved, ticked rim.   Type uncertain.
> *Dimension:* Greatest diameter, 19.6 cm.
> *Provenience:* San Cosmos, Arizona.

FIGURE 5: No. 81843
> *Description:* Pitcher.
> *Dimension:* Greatest height, 13.8 cm.
> *Provenience:* Roosevelt, Arizona (Roosevelt 9:12).   Gift of Gila Pueblo.

FIGURE 6: No. 75029
> *Description:* Jar; concave base.
> *Dimension:* Greatest height, 11.1 cm.
> *Provenience:* Round Valley, Arizona.

1

2

3

4

5

6

PLATE 124: ROOSEVELT BLACK-ON-WHITE
Salado Branch

FIGURE 1: No. 75103
>*Description:* Miniature pitcher. Type uncertain.
>*Dimension:* Greatest height, 6.9 cm.
>*Provenience:* Taylor, Arizona.

FIGURE 2: No. 74575
>*Description:* Pitcher; twisted handle.
>*Dimension:* Greatest height, 9.8 cm.
>*Provenience:* Ojo Caliente, New Mexico.

FIGURE 3: No. 75139
>*Description:* Miniature pitcher. Type uncertain.
>*Dimension:* Greatest height, 5.9 cm.
>*Provenience:* Mesa Redonda, Arizona.

FIGURE 4: No. 73857
>*Description:* Ladle. Type uncertain.
>*Dimension:* Greatest diameter of bowl, 7 cm.
>*Provenience:* San Cosmos, Arizona.

FIGURE 5: No. 75079
>*Description:* Ladle.
>*Dimension:* Greatest length, 20.5 cm.
>*Provenience:* Round Valley, Arizona.

FIGURE 6: No. 81628
>*Description:* Ladle.
>*Dimension:* Greatest length, 24.4 cm.
>*Provenience:* Roosevelt Lake, Arizona (Arizona C:5:13). Exchange with Gila Pueblo.

FIGURE 7: No. 75171
>*Description:* Ladle. Type uncertain.
>*Dimension:* Greatest length, 13.4 cm.
>*Provenience:* Mesa Redonda, Arizona.

FIGURE 8: No. 75152
>*Description:* Canteen; one of two mushroom handles missing.
>*Dimension:* Greatest height, 9.5 cm.
>*Provenience:* Mesa Redonda, Arizona.

FIGURE 9: No. 74589
>*Description:* Pitcher.
>*Dimension:* Greatest height, 13.7 cm.
>*Provenience:* Ojo Caliente, New Mexico.

FIGURE 10: No. 74151
>*Description:* Bowl. Type uncertain.
>*Dimension:* Greatest diameter, 12.1 cm.
>*Provenience:* San Cosmos, Arizona.

PLATE 125: POLYCHROMES OF THE SALADO BRANCH

FIGURE 1: No. 75162

Description: Bowl; Pinto Polychrome.
Dimension: Greatest diameter, 21.7 cm.
Provenience: Mesa Redonda, Arizona.

FIGURE 2: No. 81682

Description: Bowl; Pinto Polychrome.
Dimension: Greatest diameter, 24.6 cm.
Provenience: Roosevelt Lake, Arizona (Roosevelt 5:10).　Exchange with Gila Pueblo.

FIGURE 3: No. 75173

Description: Bowl; Pinto Polychrome.
Dimension: Greatest diameter, 17.8 cm.
Provenience: Mesa Redonda, Arizona.

FIGURE 4: No. 74777

Description: Bowl; single horizontal handle.　Pinto Polychrome.
Dimension: Greatest diameter, excluding handle, 14.1 cm.
Provenience: X Ranch, Arizona.

FIGURE 5: No. 74849

Description: Bowl; Pinto Polychrome.
Dimension: Greatest diameter, 16.6 cm.
Provenience: Ojo Bonito, New Mexico.

FIGURE 6: No. 74022

Description: Jar; Tonto Polychrome.
Dimension: Greatest height, 12.5 cm.
Provenience: San Cosmos, Arizona.

FIGURE 7: No. 81608

Description: Bowl; Gila Polychrome.
Dimension: Greatest diameter, 28.1 cm.
Provenience: Near Roosevelt Lake, Arizona (Roosevelt 5:9).　Exchange with Gila
    Pueblo.

FIGURE 8: No. 81846

Description: Bowl; Tonto Polychrome.
Dimension: Greatest diameter, 16 cm.
Provenience: Roosevelt, Arizona (Roosevelt 5:10).　Gift of Gila Pueblo.

BIBLIOGRAPHY
BY CHAPTERS

I. KAYENTA BRANCH
Caywood and Spicer, 1935
Colton, 1932; 1939
Colton and Hargrave, 1937
Fewkes, 1898; 1904
Gladwin, 1934, fig. 7
Hargrave, 1932
Hawley, 1936
Kidder, 1924, pp. 68, 89
Morss, 1931

II. MESA VERDE BRANCH
Gladwin, 1934, fig. 8
Hawley, 1936
Kidder, 1924, p. 58
Martin, Lloyd, and Spoehr, 1938
Martin and Rinaldo, 1939
Martin, Roys, and von Bonin, 1936
Morris, 1928; 1939
Roberts, 1930

III. CHACO BRANCH
Gladwin, 1931; 1934, fig. 4
Hawley, 1934; 1936

Kidder, 1924, p. 49
Pepper, 1920
Roberts, 1931; 1932

IV. CIBOLA BRANCH
Colton, 1937
Fewkes, 1904; 1909
Gladwin, 1931; 1934, fig. 3
Haury, 1934
Haury and Hargrave, 1931
Hawley, 1936
Hodge, 1923; 1924
Kidder, 1924, pp. 89, 96
Kidder and Shepard, 1936
Mera, 1934
Morris, 1928
Nesbitt, 1938
Roberts, 1932
Spier, 1919; 1919a

V. SALADO BRANCH
Gladwin, 1930; 1931; 1934, fig. 5
Hawley, 1936
Kidder, 1924, p. 105

271

BIBLIOGRAPHY

BONIN, GERHARDT VON.   See MARTIN, PAUL S., ROYS, LAWRENCE, and VON BONIN, GERHARDT

CAYWOOD, LOUIS R., and SPICER, EDWARD H.
    1935.   Tuzigoot: The excavation and repair of a ruin on the Verde River near Clark-dale, Arizona.   Field Division of Education, National Park Service.   Berkeley, California.

COLTON, HAROLD S.
    1932.   A survey of prehistoric sites in the region of Flagstaff, Arizona.   Bureau of American Ethnology, Bulletin 104.   Washington, D.C.
    1939.   The reducing atmosphere and oxidizing atmosphere in prehistoric southwestern ceramics.   American Antiquity, vol. 4, No. 3.   Menasha, Wisconsin.

———, and HARGRAVE, LYNDON L.
    1937.   Handbook of northern Arizona pottery wares.   Museum of Northern Arizona, Bulletin 11.   Flagstaff, Arizona.

FEWKES, JESSE W.
    1898.   Archaeological expedition to Arizona in 1895.   17th Annual Report, Bureau of American Ethnology.   Washington, D.C.
    1904.   Two summers' work in pueblo ruins.   22nd Annual Report, Bureau of American Ethnology.   Washington, D.C.
    1909.   Ancient Zuñi pottery.   Putnam Anniversary Volume.   New York.

GLADWIN, WINIFRED and HAROLD S.
    1930.   Some southwestern pottery types, Series 1.   Medallion Papers No. 8.   Globe, Arizona.
    1930a.   A method for the designation of southwestern pottery types.   Medallion Papers No. 7.   Globe, Arizona.
    1931.   Some southwestern pottery types, Series II.   Medallion Papers No. 10.   Globe, Arizona.
    1934.   A method for designation of cultures and their variations.   Medallion Papers No. 15.   Globe, Arizona.

GUERNSEY, SAMUEL J.   See KIDDER, ALFRED V., and GUERNSEY, SAMUEL J.

HARGRAVE, LYNDON L.
    1932.   Guide to forty pottery types from the Hopi country and the San Francisco Mountains, Arizona.   Museum of Northern Arizona, Bulletin 1.   Flagstaff, Arizona.
    See COLTON, HAROLD S., and HARGRAVE, LYNDON L.
    See HAURY, EMIL W., and HARGRAVE, LYNDON L.

HAURY, EMIL W.
    1930.   A sequence of decorated redware from the Silver Creek drainage.   Museum of Northern Arizona.   Museum Notes, vol. 2, No. 11.   Flagstaff, Arizona.
    1934.   The Canyon Creek ruin and the cliff dwellings of the Sierra Ancha.   Medallion Papers No. 14.   Globe, Arizona.

———, and HARGRAVE, LYNDON L.
    1931.   Recently dated pueblo ruins in Arizona.   Smithsonian Miscellaneous Collections, vol. 82, No. 11.   Washington, D.C.

HAWLEY, FLORENCE M.

1934. The significance of the dated prehistory of Chetro Ketl, Chaco Canyon, New Mexico. University of New Mexico Bulletin No. 246. Albuquerque, New Mexico.

1936. Field manual of prehistoric southwestern pottery types. University of New Mexico Bulletin No. 291. Albuquerque, New Mexico.

HODGE, FREDERICK W.

1923. Circular kivas near Hawikuh. Contributions from the Museum of the American Indian, Heye Foundation, vol. 7, No. 1. New York.

1924. Pottery of Hawikuh. Indian Notes, Museum of the American Indian, Heye Foundation, vol. 1, pp. 8–15. New York.

HOUGH, WALTER

1903. Archaeological field work in northeastern Arizona: The Museum-Gates Expedition of 1901. United States National Museum, Annual Report for 1901, pp. 279–358. Washington, D.C.

1930. Explorations of ruins in the White Mountain Apache Indian Reservation, Arizona. Proceedings of the United States National Museum, vol. 78, art. 13, pp. 1–21. Washington, D.C.

KIDDER, ALFRED V.

1924. An introduction to the study of southwestern archaeology. Papers of the Southwestern Expedition, No. 1. Phillips Academy, Andover, Massachusetts. New Haven, Connecticut.

———, and GUERNSEY, SAMUEL J.

1919. Archaeological explorations in northeastern Arizona. Bureau of American Ethnology, Bulletin 65. Washington, D.C.

———, and SHEPARD, ANNA O.

1936. The pottery of Pecos, vol. 2. Papers of the Southwestern Expedition, No. 7. Phillips Academy, Andover, Massachusetts. New Haven, Connecticut.

LLOYD, CARL. See MARTIN, PAUL S., LLOYD, CARL, and SPOEHR, ALEXANDER

MAERZ, A., and PAUL, M. REA

1930. A dictionary of color. New York.

MARTIN, PAUL S., ROYS, LAWRENCE, and VON BONIN, GERHARDT

1936. Lowry Ruin in southwestern Colorado. Field Museum of Natural History, Anthropological Series, vol. 23, No. 1.

MARTIN, PAUL S., LLOYD, CARL, and SPOEHR, ALEXANDER

1938. Archaeological field work in the Ackmen-Lowry area, southwestern Colorado, 1937. Field Museum of Natural History, Anthropological Series, vol. 23, No. 2.

MARTIN, PAUL S., and RINALDO, JOHN

1939. Modified Basket Maker sites, Ackmen-Lowry region, southwestern Colorado. Field Museum of Natural History, Anthropological Series, vol. 23, No. 3.

MERA, H. P.

1934. Observations on the archaeology of the Petrified Forest National Monument. Laboratory of Anthropology, Technical Series, Bulletin No. 7. Santa Fe, New Mexico.

MORRIS, EARL H.
    1928. The Aztec Ruin. American Museum of Natural History, Anthropological Papers, vol. 26. New York.

————, and SHEPARD, ANNA O.
    1939. Archaeological studies in the La Plata District. Carnegie Institution of Washington. Washington, D.C.

MORSS, NOEL
    1931. Notes on the archaeology of the Kaibito and Rainbow Plateaus in Arizona. Papers of the Peabody Museum of American Archaeology and Ethnology, vol. 12, No. 2, Harvard University. Cambridge, Massachusetts.

NESBITT, PAUL H.
    1938. Starkweather Ruin. Logan Museum Publications in Anthropology, Bulletin No. 6. Beloit, Wisconsin.

PEPPER, GEORGE H.
    1920. Pueblo Bonito. American Museum of Natural History, Anthropological Papers, vol. 27. New York.

PRUDDEN, T. MITCHELL
    1903. The prehistoric ruins of the San Juan watershed in Utah, Arizona, Colorado, and New Mexico. American Anthropologist, n.s., vol. 5. Lancaster, Pennsylvania.

RINALDO, JOHN. See MARTIN, PAUL S., and RINALDO, JOHN

ROBERTS, FRANK H. H., JR.
    1930. Early pueblo ruins in the Piedra district, southwestern Colorado. Bureau of American Ethnology, Bulletin No. 96. Washington, D.C.
    1931. The ruins at Kiatuthlanna. Bureau of American Ethnology, Bulletin No. 100. Washington, D.C.
    1932. The village of the great kivas on the Zuñi Reservation. Bureau of American Ethnology, Bulletin No. 111. Washington, D.C.

ROYS, LAWRENCE. See MARTIN, PAUL S., ROYS, LAWRENCE, and VON BONIN, GERHARDT

SAYLES, E. B.
    1936. Some southwestern pottery types, Series V. Medallion Papers No. 21. Globe, Arizona.

SHEPARD, ANNA O. See KIDDER, ALFRED V., and SHEPARD, ANNA O.; also MORRIS, EARL H., and SHEPARD, ANNA O.

SPICER, EDWARD H. See CAYWOOD, LOUIS R., and SPICER, EDWARD H.

SPIER, LESLIE
    1919. An outline for a chronology of Zuñi ruins. American Museum of Natural History, Anthropological Papers, vol. 18, part 3. New York.
    1919a. Notes on some Little Colorado ruins. American Museum of Natural History, Anthropological Papers, vol. 18, part 4. New York.

SPOEHR, ALEXANDER. See MARTIN, PAUL S., LLOYD, CARL, and SPOEHR, ALEXANDER

SITES REPRESENTED BY ILLUSTRATED POTTERY TYPES

Site	Plate Number	Pottery Type
Ackmen, Colorado	57	Abajo Red-on-Orange La Plata Black-on-Orange
Allantown, Arizona (vicinity of)	12	Tusayan Black-on-White
Awatovi, Arizona	39, 43	Jeddito Black-on-Yellow
	47	Bidahochi Polychrome
	48, 50, 51, 55	Sikyatki Polychrome
Bidahochi, Arizona	4	Kana-a Black-on-White
	8	Black Mesa Black-on-White
	20	Bidahochi Black-on-White
	27, 28	Jeddito Black-on-Orange
	32	Jeddito Black-on-Yellow
	46	Bidahochi Polychrome
	110	Pseudo Black-on-White
	118, 120	Zuñi Glazes
Blue Canyon, Arizona	2, 3	Kana-a Black-on-White
	15	Tusayan Polychrome
Bug Canyon, Utah	58, 59	Mancos Black-on-White
Canyon Diablo, Arizona	8	Black Mesa Black-on-White
Chaco Canyon, New Mexico	3	Kana-a Black-on-White
	6, 7	Black Mesa Black-on-White
	12	Tusayan Black-on-White
	14	Tusayan Black-on-Red
	17, 18	Sagi Black-on-White
	57	La Plata Black-on-Orange
	58	Mancos Black-on-White
	61	McElmo Black-on-White
	64, 65	Kiatuthlanna Black-on-White
	66, 67	Red Mesa Black-on-White
	68, 69	Chaco Black-on-White
	73	Puerco Black-on-White
	92	Wingate Black-on-Red
Chevellon Buttes, Arizona (and vicinity)	35	Jeddito Black-on-Yellow
	111	Painted and corrugated
	115	Homolovi Polychrome
Chukubi, Arizona	2	Kana-a Black-on-White
	37, 39	Jeddito Black-on-Yellow
	48	Sikyatki Polychrome
Cortez, Colorado (vicinity of)	57	La Plata Black-on-Orange
Eagar, Arizona; see Round Valley, Arizona		
Flagstaff, Arizona (vicinity of)	16	Sagi Black-on-White
	121	Snowflake Black-on-White

Site	Plate Number	Pottery Type
Gallup, New Mexico (vicinity of)	66	Red Mesa Black-on-White
Hard Scrabble, Arizona	71	Puerco Black-on-White
	78	Reserve Black-on-White
	118	Zuñi Glazes
Holbrook, Arizona (vicinity of)	2, 3	Kana-a Black-on-White
	78	Reserve Black-on-White
	121	Snowflake Black-on-White
Homolovi (No. 1), Arizona	1	Four Mile Polychrome
	5	Black Mesa Black-on-White
	10	Tusayan Black-on-White
	16, 17, 19	Sagi Black-on-White
	20–23	Bidahochi Black-on-White
	24–29	Jeddito Black-on-Orange
	30–35, 38–43	Jeddito Black-on-Yellow
	44–47	Bidahochi Polychrome
	51	Sikyatki Polychrome
	81	Tularosa Black-on-White
	94	Wingate Black-on-Red
	101	St. Johns Polychrome
	103, 104	Pinedale Polychrome
	105–108	Four Mile Polychrome
	109	Showlow Polychrome
	110	Pseudo Black-on-White
	112–117	Homolovi Polychrome
	119	Zuñi Glazes
Homolovi (No. 2), Arizona	12	Tusayan Black-on-White
	30–37, 40, 43	Jeddito Black-on-Yellow
	44	Bidahochi Polychrome
	105, 106, 108	Four Mile Polychrome
	109	Showlow Polychrome
	113, 117	Homolovi Polychrome
	119, 120	Zuñi Glazes
Hopi Buttes, Arizona	13	Tusayan Black-on-White
Houck, Arizona	69	Chaco Black-on-White
Kishuba, Arizona	4	Kana-a Black-on-White
	7, 8	Black Mesa Black-on-White
	11	Tusayan Black-on-White
	15	Kayenta and Kiet Siel Polychromes
	17, 19	Sagi Black-on-White
La Plata River, New Mexico (mouth of)	62, 63	Mesa Verde Black-on-White
Lowry Ruin, Colorado (and vicinity)	58, 59	Mancos Black-on-White
	60, 61	McElmo Black-on-White
	62, 63	Mesa Verde Black-on-White

Site	Plate Number	Pottery Type
McElmo Canyon, Colorado, and Utah....................	56............	Post-Conquest
	60............	McElmo Black-on-White
	15............	Kiet Siel Polychrome
	64............	Kiatuthlanna Black-on-White
	71............	Puerco Black-on-White
	75............	Reserve Black-on-White
Mesa Redonda, Arizona.........	93, 97........	Wingate Black-on-Red
	99............	St. Johns Polychrome
	111...........	McDonald Corrugated
	121, 122.......	Snowflake Black-on-White
	123, 124.......	Roosevelt Black-on-White
	125...........	Pinto Polychrome
	4.............	Kana-a Black-on-White
	5, 6..........	Black Mesa Black-on-White
Mishongnovi, Arizona...........	26............	Jeddito Black-on-Orange
	31–37, 39–41....	Jeddito Black-on-Yellow
	48, 51–53......	Sikyatki Polychrome
Montezuma County, Colorado.......	60............	McElmo Black-on-White
Nanapii, Arizona..................	40............	Jeddito Black-on-Yellow
Navajo Canyon, Arizona...........	7.............	Black Mesa Black-on-White

New Ackmen, Colorado; see Pleasant View, Colorado

Site	Plate Number	Pottery Type
	57............	Abajo Red-on-Orange
	64............	Kiatuthlanna Black-on-White
	67............	Red Mesa Black-on-White
	77, 80.........	Reserve Black-on-White
Ojo Bonito, New Mexico.........	85, 86.........	Tularosa Black-on-White
	91, 92, 94, 95, 98...........	Wingate Black-on-Red
	104...........	Pinedale Polychrome
	118–120.......	Zuñi Glazes
	125...........	Pinto Polychrome
	5.............	Black Mesa Black-on-White
	16, 18.........	Sagi Black-on-White
	64, 65.........	Kiatuthlanna Black-on-White
	66............	Red Mesa Black-on-White
	71, 73.........	Puerco Black-on-White
Ojo Caliente, New Mexico........	74............	Puerco Black-on-Red
	76, 78, 79......	Reserve Black-on-White
	83, 84.........	Tularosa Black-on-White
	92............	Wingate Black-on-Red
	101...........	St. Johns Polychrome
	118, 120.......	Zuñi Glazes
	124...........	Roosevelt Black-on-White

Site	Plate Number	Pottery Type
Old Walpi, Arizona	4	Kana-a Black-on-White
	7	Black Mesa Black-on-White
	12	Tusayan Black-on-White
	14	Tusayan Black-on-Red
	19	Sagi Black-on-White
	31, 32, 36, 38, 39, 42, 43	Jeddito Black-on-Yellow
	48–51, 53, 55	Sikyatki Polychrome
	56	Post-Conquest
	62	Mesa Verde Black-on-White
Oraibi, Arizona (and vicinity)	2, 4	Kana-a Black-on-White
	5, 7, 9	Black Mesa Black-on-White
	11	Tusayan Black-on-White
	14	Tusayan Black-on-Red
	16	Sagi Black-on-White
	39, 43	Jeddito Black-on-Yellow
	50, 51, 53, 55	Sikyatki Polychrome
	56	Post-Conquest
Oraibi Wash, Arizona	8	Black Mesa Black-on-White
	15	Kiet Siel Polychrome
	17	Sagi Black-on-White
	23	Bidahochi Black-on-White
Payupki, Arizona	5	Black Mesa Black-on-White
	56	Post-Conquest
Pleasant View, Colorado	57	Abajo Red-on-Orange / La Plata Black-on-Orange
	59	Mancos Black-on-White
	60	McElmo Black-on-White
Pueblo Alto, Chaco Canyon, New Mexico	68, 69	Chaco Black-on-White
Roosevelt, Roosevelt Lake, Arizona (and vicinity)	123, 124	Roosevelt Black-on-White
	125	Pinto, Gila, and Tonto Polychromes
Round Valley, Arizona	70, 72, 73	Puerco Black-on-White
	74	Puerco Black-on-Red
	75–80	Reserve Black-on-White
	82–86, 88	Tularosa Black-on-White
	91–93, 95, 96	Wingate Black-on-Red
	102	Querino Polychrome
	121, 122	Snowflake Black-on-White
	123, 124	Roosevelt Black-on-White
St. Johns, Arizona (vicinity of)	77	Reserve Black-on-White
	121	Snowflake Black-on-White

Site	Plate Number	Pottery Type
	6	Black Mesa Black-on-White
	11	Tusayan Black-on-White
	64	Kiatuthlanna Black-on-White
	70–72	Puerco Black-on-White
	74	Puerco Black-on-Red
	79, 80	Reserve Black-on-White
	81–88	Tularosa Black-on-White
	89–98	Wingate Black-on-Red
San Cosmos, Arizona	99–101	St. Johns Polychrome
	102	Houck and Querino Polychromes
	103	Pinedale Polychrome
	105	Four Mile Polychrome
	110	Pseudo Black-on-White
	118–120	Zuñi Glazes
	122	Snowflake Black-on-White
	123, 124	Roosevelt Black-on-White
	125	Tonto Polychrome
San Juan River, Utah	61	McElmo Black-on-White
	62, 63	Mesa Verde Black-on-White
Shipaulovi, Arizona	3	Kana-a Black-on-White
	2	Kana-a Black-on-White
Shungopovi, Arizona	34, 38, 41	Jeddito Black-on-Yellow
	47	Bidahochi Polychrome
	48	Sikyatki Polychrome
	6	Black Mesa Black-on-White
Sikyatki, Arizona	35–38, 40–42	Jeddito Black-on-Yellow
	48–54	Sikyatki Polychrome
	110	Pseudo Black-on-White
Starkweather Ruin, New Mexico	75	Reserve Black-on-White
Taylor, Arizona	124	Roosevelt Black-on-White
Tohatchi, New Mexico (vicinity of)	69	Chaco Black-on-White
	122	Snowflake Black-on-White
Walpi; see Old Walpi, Arizona		
	104	Pinedale Polychrome
White River, Arizona	108	Four Mile Polychrome
	111	McDonald Corrugated
Wingate, New Mexico (vicinity of)	68	Chaco Black-on-White
	6	Black Mesa Black-on-White
	12	Tusayan Black-on-White
	15	Kiet Siel Polychrome
X Ranch, Arizona	16, 18, 19	Sagi Black-on-White
	22	Bidahochi Black-on-White
	79	Reserve Black-on-White
	93, 96, 98	Wingate Black-on-Red
	125	Pinto Polychrome

CATALOGUE NUMBERS AND COLLECTORS

Catalogue Number	Collector
21044–21201	T. V. Keam
21225–21264	Henry Hales
21394–21438	C. H. Green
21742–21756	W. K. Moorehead
21791	P. Stauffer
44217–44218	H. R. Voth
45292–47638	Paul S. Martin
47769–47770	Paul S. Martin
52654–52763	Geo. A. Dorsey
66626–67231	H. R. Voth
72018–75286	F. J. Wattron
75395–81422	Chas. L. Owen
81502–81599	Richard Wetherill
81608–81630	H. S. Gladwin
81655–81662	Earl H. Morris

Catalogue Number	Collector
81682–81690	H. S. Gladwin
81795–81837	Richard Wetherill
81843–81864	H. S. Gladwin
81925–82002	J. A. Burt
82004–82036	J. A. Burt
82083	Paul H. Nesbitt
84770–84771	Chas. L. Owen
92410	F. W. Starr
111441	Chas. F. Gunther
111208	Unknown
111617	Mr. and Mrs. Wm. Haskell Simpson
167972	Mr. E. E. Ayer
205992–206001	F. F. McArthur
206286–206335	Paul S. Martin

INDEX

Names of sub-types, synonyms for illustrated types, type-names used in this volume, and authorities.

281

Type	Authority and Date	Plate Number
Flagstaff Black-on-White	Colton and Hargrave, 1937	

Probably included in Tusayan Black-
on-White

Fugitive Red. Mentioned in caption, Plate 4		
Gallup Black-on-White	Hawley, 1936	

Probably included in Red Mesa
Black-on-White

Gila Polychrome	Kidder, 1924	125
Hawikuh Glaze B	Hodge, 1923	

See Heshotauthla Polychrome

Hawikuh Glaze C	Hodge, 1923	

See Hawikuh Glaze-on-White

Hawikuh Glaze D	Hodge, 1923	

See Arauca Polychrome

Hawikuh Glaze III	Hodge, 1924	

See Wallace Polychrome

Hawikuh Glaze-on-White	Colton and Hargrave, 1937	119
Heshotauthla Polychrome	Kidder and Shepard, 1936	118
Holbrook Black-on-White	Mera, 1934	

Probably included in Black Mesa
Black-on-White

Homolovi Polychrome	Mera, 1934	112–117
Hopi Black-on-Orange	Gladwin, 1934	

See Jeddito Black-on-Orange

Houck Polychrome	Roberts, 1932	102
Hoyapi Black-on-White	Colton and Hargrave, 1937	

Probably included in Sagi Black-on-
White

Jeddito Black-on-Orange	Haury and Hargrave, 1931	24–29
Jeddito Black-on-Yellow	Haury and Hargrave, 1931	30–43
Jeddito Brown-on-Yellow	Gladwin, 1930a	

See Jeddito Black-on-Yellow

Jeddito Engraved	Colton and Hargrave, 1937	

Included in Jeddito Black-on-Yellow

Jeddito Stippled	Colton and Hargrave, 1937	

Included in Jeddito Black-on-Yellow

Kana-a Black-on-White	Hargrave, 1932	2–4
Kayenta Polychrome	Kidder, 1924	15
Kayenta Black-on-White	Kidder, 1924	

See Sagi Black-on-White

Kia-ko Black-on-White	Colton and Hargrave, 1937	

Probably included in Tusayan Black-
on-White

Kiatuthlanna Black-on-White	Gladwin, 1934	64–65
Kiet Siel Polychrome	Colton and Hargrave, 1937	15